BEAT THE ODDS

J. Edward Allen

- Gambling Research Institute -
Cardoza Publishing

Cardoza Publishing is the foremost gaming and gambling publisher in the world with a library of close to
100 up-to-date and easy-to-read books and strategies.
These authoritative works are written by the top experts
in their fields and with more than 6,500,000 books in
print, represent the best-selling and most popular gaming
books anywhere.

Fourth Edition

Copyright © 1984, 1993, 1997, 2003 by Cardoza Publishing
- All Rights Reserved -

ISBN: 1-58042-066-4
Library of Congress Catalog No.: 2002104553

Visit our new web site or write us
for a full list of Cardoza books and strategies.

CARDOZA PUBLISHING
PO Box 1500 Cooper Station, New York, NY 10276
Phone (800)577-WINS
email: cardozapub@aol.com
www.cardozapub.com

Table of Contents

Introduction

Learn to beat the odds! If you want to gamble, then you should be as well informed as possible. The information in this book will enable you to make the best bets and play the best strategies. Instead of playing *against* the odds, you'll play like a winner. And that's what this book is all about—playing to win!

You will learn not only the fundamentals of playing and winning at all the forms of gambling we cover, but also, money management and self-control. Those methods allow you to play like a pro and retain your winnings. There's a wealth of knowledge in this book, and the goal is to make you a respected player and a winner.

All the sections are written in an easy-to-understand style, and are fully illustrated with pictures, tables and charts, so that any beginner, novice or experienced player can follow the information presented to beat the odds.

The first game we cover is **blackjack**, by

far the most popular of the table games offered by the casino. The reason for this popularity is simple: it's the only game in the house where the player can have an edge over the casino.

We cover the basic strategies necessary to master the game. Our strategies, based on computer studies, point the way for you to become a professional blackjack player.

Our second game, **craps**, is certainly the fastest and most exciting of the casino table games. There is action on every roll of the dice, and it's a game in which you can let loose and show your emotions openly, especially when things are going green, and winnings are piling onto winnings.

We cover the game simply and clearly, so that you fully understand how to play craps, the best bets to make, and which wagers should be avoided at all costs.

Video Poker has become the latest casino craze because skill is involved and proper play can make one a winner. In our comprehensive coverage we'll show you how to play the various types of machines, the different options you have available, and the best strategies to follow to beat the video poker machines!

You'll learn all there is to know about

video poker. This section is full of information, facts, and figures to make you a competent player and a winner at this exciting new game.

The next game we cover, **poker,** combines skill, luck and psychology, and may be the greatest game invented by man. Best of all, it can be played in a card club, casino, or privately, and once you have mastered the game, there is nothing but money to be made.

We discuss the most popular of the poker games—**7 Card Stud**, **Lowball**, **Draw Poker** and **Texas Hold'em.** After reading this section, you'll be able to go out and hold your own against top players.

Keno is a game that has attracted millions of players for a very good reason. With just a small bet, less than a dollar in most cases, and some luck, a player can walk away with thousands of dollars, and might even hit that $50,000 payoff.

We'll show you all the different bets that can be made in keno, a number of which only the top pros know about, and you'll soon see why millions are attracted to this game.

In our section on **slots**, you'll learn how to play the game for the best odds and what machines to choose. You'll also read a full history of the slot machine. You'll find out how odds are figured and how slots are set up in a casino so that the information in this book can be used to your advantage.

We reveal inside information on slots so that after reading this section, you'll not only be an informed player, but a winner as well.

The last game covered, **roulette**, has fascinated and intrigued millions of players over the years. It's not only a leisurely game to play, but an exciting one as well. You'll be able to play roulette in the same manner as kings, queens, statesmen and millionaires have over the years.

Roulette has a great variety of bets available, and we discuss all of them in detail. Both the American and European game are fully covered so that no matter where you find yourself, you can make the best bets at this ancient and interesting game. And with a little luck, you may come home with big winnings.

Let's beat the odds!

Winning Blackjack

Introduction

Blackjack's popularity continues to grow, and it is by far the most popular of the table games the casino offers. The reason for this is simple: the possibility of having an edge over the casino is thrilling to all players.

In order to have this edge, the player must know basic strategy and play this strategy correctly. This is not difficult to do, and it's all here in this guide—everything the player must know to play at his best and to beat the house.

The strategies shown in this book are based upon computer studies and should be examined carefully. They're explained in such a way that anyone, after a few hours or less of practice, can be winner at this popular and exciting casino game.

The Blackjack Scene

The area devoted to blackjack in any casino will usually be the largest area devoted to any of the table games. This includes not only blackjack, but also craps, roulette and baccarat. In fact, in many casinos the game is so popular that several areas may offer the game of blackjack.

It's not hard to find a game when entering the casino. There will be a number of tables placed so that they surround a center area from which the casino personnel operate. This is known as the **blackjack pit**.

The Table

The blackjack table is a modified oval, with the seats arranged around the curved position. There will be as many seats available as spots on the table.

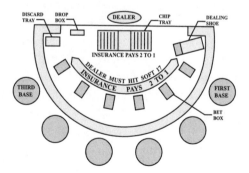

WINNING BLACKJACK

The number of seats available at a black-jack table ranges from five to seven, depending upon the casino. While the players remain seated throughout the game (unless they wish to stand) the dealer stands and faces them from the inside of the pit.

Directly in front of the dealer is the chip rack, containing the casino chips. To his right (sometimes to his left) is a slot where cash is dropped when players come to the table and change cash for chips. Also, there may be a **shoe** on the table, which is a rectangular box, either made of plastic or wood, that holds at least four decks of cards. If the game is played with only one or two decks, there will not be a shoe on the table.

There may also be a small sign stating the minimum bet (and sometimes the maximum one) permitted at the table. Sometimes this small sign shows additional rules, other than those imprinted on the green felt covering the table.

The green felt contains boxes where each player will place his chips for betting purposes, and where usually two or three rules of the game are printed. The most common is *Dealer Must Draw to 16, and Stand on All 17s,* which refers to the totals of the points the dealer holds. The next most common rule is *Insur-*

ance Pays 2-1. The third is *Blackjack Pays 3-2*.

These are very basic rules that we need not concern ourselves with right now; they will be fully explained at the appropriate time.

The Dealer

Unlike the players, the dealer stands throughout the game, and wears the house uniform. In these days of tighter security, there is usually some nametag and sometimes a picture of the dealer attached, so that the players can, by looking closely, ascertain the name of the dealer.

The dealer runs the game. He changes cash into chips issued by the casino; he **changes color**—that is, changes casino chips into smaller or larger denominations. He shuffles the cards and deals them out. He pays off winning bets and collects losing bets. He answers the players' questions, and is there to help them, as well as run the game.

Tipping the Dealer

Tipping, or **toking** the dealer is not required, but is often done. Some players over-tip; others never tip at all; and some, don't tip correctly.

A dealer should be toked if you feel that

he or she has been friendly and helpful, and has made your game more enjoyable. In that case, every now and then you can make a bet for the dealer by putting out a chip above your box in the area marked for insurance bets.

When you do this, if you win your bet, the dealer will win his; if you lose, the dealer will also lose. The dealers prefer this kind of toking, for it gives them the chance to double the original bet, and sometimes win even more if the player is dealt a blackjack.

Sometimes players tip after a blackjack is dealt to them, but one must remember that no matter how generous you want to be, your edge at blackjack is very slight, and overtipping will erode your winnings. Strike a happy balance, but under no circumstances tip a hostile or unfriendly dealer, or one who wants you to lose and considers you a sucker for playing.

The Casino Chips

Casino personnel call chips **checks**, but I will refer to them as chips throughout this book because it's the most popular term, understood by all players.

These are issued by a casino in standard denominations, usually for $1, $5, $25 and $100. Some casinos have $500 and even higher denomination chips, and many casinos have 50¢ chips at the blackjack table because payoffs are often in this amount. There are casinos that don't bother issuing chips this small, and instead pay off with coins, either half-dollars or quarters. In some of the Northern Nevada casinos, $2.50 chips are used at the blackjack tables, saving the dealers time and trouble when payoffs for $5 blackjacks are made. A blackjack, which will be explained later, pays 3-2, so a $5 wager will be paid off with $7.50.

Players can also play with cash, but casino executives frown upon this. Some players like to play only in cash, but if they win they'll have to settle for casino chips as the payoff. Dealers will always pay off in casino chips, not in cash.

Casinos have minimum betting limits, which are usually $1 or $2. Some tables may have $5 or $25 or even higher minimum limits because *high rollers* don't want to be betting thousands while some other player is betting $2 at a time.

After you leave a table, you can cash in your casino chips at the **cashier's cage** of the casino. If you don't spot it, any security guard or other casino personnel will show you where it is. That's where you get cash for your chips, not at the blackjack table.

The Players

Even though there may be five to seven spots open for players at any blackjack table, the game will begin if just one player shows up to play. When more than one player is at a table, additional players can take any of the vacant seats. There is no set rule where one is to sit.

The cards are dealt, as we shall see, in a clockwise fashion so that the player to the dealer's left, facing him, is the first player to receive cards. He is known as the **first baseman**. The player at the other end of the table, nearest to the dealer's right, is the last player to receive cards, and he's known as the **third baseman** or **anchorman**.

Where should one sit at a table if given the choice? Most experts prefer either the third baseman's seat or the one to its right, since they get a look at the other hands before making any playing decisions.

If you're a beginner, don't sit in the third baseman's seat: you might feel too much pressure, for sometimes when you draw a card you'll inadvertently make the dealer a winner. Even though you made the right decision, ignorant players may unfairly blame you for their losses. As you become more of an expert, sit as close to the third baseman's seat as you can, since you get extra information playing last.

Players in casino blackjack play their hands as individuals, trying to beat the dealer, not each other. When you are dealt cards, all you want to do is get a better hand than the dealer, in order to win. The other hands are immaterial to this result, and often some players at the table will win a hand while others will be losing their hands.

The Cards and Rules of Play

The Cards

A standard deck of fifty-two cards is used in the game of casino blackjack. At one time, most games were played with this single deck of cards, but today there are many multiple deck games in existence. No matter how many decks are used, whether two or eight they are merely multiples of the standard fifty-two-card deck game. Therefore, if a player is at a table where two decks are used, the dealer is using 104 cards, made up of two standard decks of fifty-two cards each.

The standard deck of cards contains four color suits: clubs, diamonds, hearts and spades. In blackjack, the suits have no material value and can be disregarded. The value of the cards is the only important factor.

Value of the Cards

Each of the four suits contains the identical thirteen cards, ranging from an Ace to a King. The cards are A, 2, 3, 4, 5, 6, 7, 8, 9, 10, J, Q and K.

In casino blackjack, the following cards are counted as 10s, and have that value for adding purposes to ascertain the total of the hand: 10, J, Q and K.

In the future, I'll refer to any of these cards as a **10-value card** or simply as a **10**. There are sixteen 10-value cards in the standard deck, and therefore these are the cards most frequently in play. All the other values consist of only four cards.

To value a card, other than the A, which we'll write about last, we simply examine the spots on the card, as well as the numerical value in the form of a number at the corners. Thus a 2 has two spots, the 3 has three, the 4 has four, and all the way up to the 9, which has 9 spots.

The A is the most powerful card in blackjack, and one of the reasons for its importance is that it can be valued, at the option of the player, as either a 1 or 11.

Blackjack is also called **21** because that is

the highest total that a player may validly hold. Any hand totaling more than 21 points is a loser, which is called a "**bust.**" The A, which can be valued at 1 or 11, sometimes prevents hands from going over 21, or "busting"—that is, losing, when it is valued as a 1.

For example, a hand containing 10-3-A is merely a 14, not a 24, because the player simply values the A as a 1. The A gives players, especially beginners, the most trouble. Often they think they've busted or lost, because they value the A as an 11 instead of as a 1. If in doubt, show the hand to the dealer and let him value it for you.

Object of the Game

When we discuss the object of the game, we write about the object from the player's standpoint. The dealer has no object to his play; he simply must follow the rules set forth by the casino, which is to stand on hands of 17 or more, and draw to all hands of 16 or less.

The object of the game, in its most simple terms, is to beat the dealer. To do this, the player can win in two ways. First of all, he must have a total higher than the dealer's total, or he must have a valid hand, of whatever total, while the dealer "busts" or goes over 21.

The player loses if his total is less than the dealer's total, or if the player busts. Once the player busts, his hand is out of play and his bet is removed. It doesn't matter to this player if the dealer subsequently busts his own hand; once the player busts, he loses.

If both the player and the dealer have the same totals in their respective hands, it's a tie, or standoff. The casino term for this is a "**push**." That's just what it is, a push. Neither the player nor the dealer win.

How does a player improve his total? To understand this concept, we first have to look at the original hand dealt to the player.

The Original Hand

The dealer, to put a round of play in motion, deals out two cards to each of the players and two cards to himself. The cards are dealt one at a time, face down, the player to the dealer's left getting the first card, and then each player after that getting a card in clockwise fashion. After each player has received one card, then the dealer gives himself a card, also face down. Then a second card is dealt to each of the players, also face down, in the same order, and the dealer gets his second card, and turns it face up.

This face up card is known as the **upcard**.

Thus, all the players see one of the dealer's cards, but the dealer sees none of the players' cards. It wouldn't matter if he saw the players' cards or not, since the dealer is bound by strict rules. In some casinos, the players' cards are dealt face up in multiple deck games.

Most players prefer to have their cards dealt face down, because it gives them the feeling that they're involved in a secret game of some sort, hiding their cards from the dealer, who couldn't care less. Most experts prefer to see all the cards dealt face up because they get a better grasp of what cards are in play and out of the deck, and this gives them a slight advantage.

The two cards the player gets at the outset of play is an original hand. The highest total he can get is 21 on an original hand—an A and a 10-value card. When a player (or dealer) gets this hand, it's known as a **blackjack**, or a **natural**. A blackjack pays 3-2 if it wins. All other winning hands pay even-money. If a dealer gets a blackjack and none of the players have a blackjack, the dealer simply wins the player's bet at even-money; he doesn't get that extra bonus.

If a player and the dealer have a blackjack, then it's a push; neither wins.

The next highest total is a 20. This is a

very strong hand, and usually a winning one, either on the part of the dealer or the player. Thereafter, the hands go down in value.

The important thing to remember is that neither a player nor a dealer can bust on the original hand. The following are some original hands and their totals:

Hand	Total
Q-5	15
9-8	17
4-8	12
10-K	20
A-8	19

Hitting and Standing

If a player wants to improve his hand, he can draw a card to that hand. This is called **hitting** or **drawing**. For example, if a player is dealt a 5-3, his total is only 8. Even if he hits the hand, he can't bust or go over 21. So he hits the hand, not worrying about busting.

If a player is dealt a 10-K, he has a total of 20. He doesn't want to hit this hand because his total is very strong, just one below the highest possible total. If he hits the hand he will bust unless he gets an A, and the odds against getting one of the four As is very high, so he stands.

Hard and Soft Totals

Any hand that doesn't contain an A is a hard hand, and the total of those **hard hands** are **hard totals**. Most of the hands dealt to either the player or the dealer will be hard hands like these.

Some examples of hard hands:

5-4, which is a hard 9.

10-5, which is a hard 15.

J-K, which is a hard 20.

There is another way to have a hard hand: to have a hand containing an A, where the A is counted as 1, not as an 11. For example, suppose the player was dealt an original hand of 10-4, and hit it and got an A. He now would have hard 15, because he must value the A as 1. If he valued it as an 11, the hand would total 25 and bust.

Other hard hands containing an A:

10-6-A, which is a hard 17.

9-4-A, which is a hard 14.

8-3-A, which is a hard 12.

Any hand, which contains an A, valued at 11, rather than as 1, is a **soft hand**, and its total is a **soft total**.

For example, suppose a player received an original hand of A-9. It would be a soft 20, with the A counted as an 11. Of course, the player would have the option of counting the hand as a 10, but that would be foolish since his 20 is very strong. If he counted it as a 10 and hit the hand, any card drawn other than an A or ten-value would weaken the hand.

Here are some examples of soft hands:

A-9 is a soft 20.

A-8 is a soft 19.

A-7 is a soft 18.

A soft hand has one important advantage. Even if the hand is hit, it can't bust. So if a foolish player hit a soft 20, consisting of an A and 9 he still couldn't bust.

A soft hand can become a hard hand, if it's drawn to. For example, if a player were dealt an A-6 for a soft 17 and hit and got an 8, his hand would not be a hard 15 (A-6-8 = 15). An A-4, which is a soft 15, if hit with a 7, would become a hard 12. The same A-4, if hit with a 5, would become a soft 20.

We'll go into the strategies of hitting or standing on soft totals later on.

The Blackjack

This is the strongest of all hands, and consists of an A and a 10-value card (10, J, Q or K) dealt as an original hand. It is an immediate winner for the player—unless the dealer has a blackjack also, in which case it is a push.

But if the dealer doesn't have a blackjack, it pays off at 3-2.

If the dealer has a blackjack and none of the players have one, then the dealer wins all the bets at the table.

As we shall see, the player has an option of splitting As and playing each A as a separate hand. If a ten-value card is dealt to a split A, it's not a blackjack, just a 21.

Remember, only an A and a 10-value card in the original hand is a blackjack.

Busting

Sometimes this is also known as breaking, but busting is the more common term used in casinos. When either a player or a dealer has drawn cards to his original hand and gone over 21, the hand is a losing one; he has busted. The only valid hands are those of 21 or fewer points.

When we bust—that is, go over 21 after hitting our hand—we must turn the cards over immediately to show that we lost, and the dealer will, at that point, take away both our cards and our chips. We've lost, and are out of the game for that round of play, even if the dealer subsequently busts. This is the big edge the casino has over us. If the dealer and the player both bust, the player still loses.

Well, then, you might ask, why would anyone risk drawing and busting a hand? As we shall see, there are times when the dealer's upcard forces us to hit our hand, even though we may bust, because he probably has a 17 or higher total, and if we stand with a stiff total, (12 to 16) we'll lose our bets without even trying to improve our hands.

Playing the Casino Game

We're now ready to see how the game is played in a casino. For purposes of this illustration, assume we enter a casino to play some 21. The first thing we do is head for the blackjack pit, looking for a table that will accommodate our wagers. If we wish to bet only $2 a hand, we must find a table with a $1 or a $2 minimum, and avoid the tables with a $5 or higher minimum.

We find several tables like that. At one table only two players are seated: one is in the first baseman's spot at the extreme left of the dealer; the other player is in the center spot. We move to the anchorman's seat, take out some cash, place it on the table, and wait for the dealer to change it into casino chips.

The dealer is about to shuffle up the cards, and so he puts them down and takes our cash.

Our involvement with casino blackjack has begun.

Changing Cash into Chips

We are already seated in the last chair when the dealer takes our cash and counts it. We had put down $40, in assorted $10s and $20s, and the dealer will turn the money over after counting it, to verify that it's not funny money with one denomination printed on the front and a different one printed on the back.

In most casinos, he'll not only verify the amount with us by announcing "forty dollars," but will also try and catch the attention of a casino executive, a floorman, who will be in the interior of the pit, supervising the games. After the floorman acknowledges that this cash amount is being exchanged for chips, the dealer will drop the cash into a slot and it will disappear from view.

Then he'll give us $40 worth of chips. Since it's a $2 table, he might give us $20 worth of $1 chips and four $5 chips. We count the chips after he gives them to us. Anyone can make a mistake, and this is perfectly acceptable behavior.

While we're doing this, the dealer is shuffling the cards.

Shuffling, Cutting and Burning a Card

In the casino we're playing at, there are both one-deck and multiple deck games, but we've sat at a table with a one-deck game. The dealer is shuffling up the cards, doing a thorough job. When he's finished, the cards are placed on the table in front of one of the players to be cut. Some players, out of superstition, refuse to cut the cards, which is also acceptable. But the player sitting in the first base cuts them by taking up a portion of the cards and placing them next to the original stack. In some casinos, a plastic card is handed to the player to be inserted somewhere in the deck, then the cards on top of the card are placed below it. Either cut is legitimate.

After the cards are cut, the dealer places them all together and then removes the top card. He either places the top card on the bottom of the deck, face up (but in such a manner that the players cannot see its value) or places it in a small plastic case to his right, face down. If he does the latter, then all future discards—cards already played out—will be placed on top of that card. If he turns the card face up at the bottom of the deck, then all future discards will be placed face up below that burned card.

The above paragraph describes what is meant by **burning a card**. This is a ritual car-

ried out in practically all casinos, and hear-
kens back to the days when the casino was
worried that someone would cut to a precise
part of the deck, and thus take advantage of
knowledge of the top card. Which still might
be done, for all we know.

Making a Bet

As the dealer holds the cards, getting ready
to deal, the players make their bets. We will
see a rectangular printed box right in front of
our seat, and this is where our chips go.

The bet must be made prior to the deal of
the cards. It must be at least the minimum allowed at the table, and cannot be more than
the maximum permitted at the table.

However, we're not thinking of $500 bets
(usually the maximum at most casinos) as we
put out two $1 chips. We're going to get our
feet wet and test the waters. Our chips are now
in our betting box, and since the other two
players have also made their bets, the dealer
is ready to deal out the cards.

The Deal

The first baseman gets the top card, face
down, then the second player gets his card,
and then we get ours. The last of the first cards
to be dealt goes to the dealer, also face down.

Now a second card goes out in the same order, but the dealer turns over this card, his upcard.

We now all have original hands of two cards, and can exercise our various options, or act upon our hands. For purposes of this illustration, we're simply going to make a decision as to whether to hit or stand.

Hitting or Standing—How To

To refresh our recollection, hitting means drawing a card to our original hand. We can hit our hand as often as we care to, so long as the total of the cards doesn't exceed 21.

To hit—that is, ask for another card—we pick up our original cards and scrape the edges on the felt surface toward us. This is the universal signal for a hit in all casinos that deal cards face down. The dealer will give you another card from the top of the stock he's holding in his hand.

If we want another card after our original hit, we scrape again. If we're satisfied with our hand, we slide the cards under our bet chips, and don't touch either the card or the chips again.

As you may have noticed, no verbal commands are given to the dealer. The whole game can be played silently with these signals.

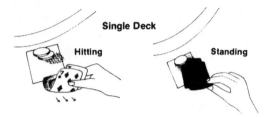

Hitting and Standing in Multiple Deck Games

When all the players' cards are dealt face up, which is the usual case in multiple deck games involving four or more decks, there are different signals used by players when they wish to hit or stand.

If a player wants to draw another card, his signal for a hit is to point his index finger at the cards. Another card will be given to him by the dealer. Or the player may scratch the felt surface of the table behind his cards with his index finger, and this is also a signal for a hit. Either signal is universally accepted in American casinos.

If that same player wants to stand with his total, he simply waves his hand over the cards, with the palm face down, and the dealer will respect this signal and pass him by.

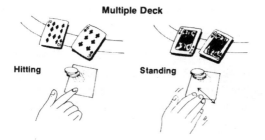

Multiple Deck

Hitting   Standing

Blackjacks

If a player is fortunate enough to be dealt a blackjack, which is an A and 10-value card dealt to him as an original hand, he turns these over immediately. If the dealer doesn't have a blackjack also, the player will be paid off at once at 3-2, and his cards will be taken out of play.

Dealer's Upcard

In single deck games, if the dealer's upcard is a 10 (or 10-value), he immediately peeks at his hole card (the face down card below the upcard) to see if he has a blackjack. If he does, he turns the A over and collects bets from all players who themselves don't have blackjacks. If he doesn't have an A in the hole, he continues dealing the game.

If the dealer has an A as an upcard, then

he will ask the players if they want insurance. This will be explained later.

Playing the Hand

Let's assume, in our theoretical game at the table with the other two players, that the dealer's upcard is a 9. He doesn't have to peek at his hole card, for there's no way he can have a blackjack with a 9 showing.

The first baseman is the first to act on his hand. Remember, the players act first—that is, hit or stand—and then the dealer acts last, after all the players have made their decisions.

The first baseman scrapes his cards for a hit. He is dealt a Q. He scrapes the cards again for another hit, and gets a 7. Disgustedly, he turns over the cards he has been holding. He had a 3 and a 2, making his original hand a 5, with the Q and 7 he now holds 22, and has busted. The dealer takes away the first baseman's chips and cards and now turns his attention to the second player.

This player scrapes for a hit, gets a 4, and then happily slides his cards under his chips, a signal that he is now standing on his total. The dealer now turns to us. We look at our cards and find we hold a J and a 9. Our 19 is a strong total, so we stand by—sliding the cards under our chips. Now it's the dealer's turn. He turns over his hole card.

His hole card was 3, giving him a total of 12. Under the rules of the game, he must hit his hand, since it totals less than 17. He takes a card for himself by putting the top card of the stock face up next to his original cards. It is a 4, giving him a 16. He must hit again. He has no options. His next card is a K. The dealer has gone over 21 and busted.

At this point, he takes the second player's original cards from under the chips and turns them over. This player had a 10 and a 6 for a 16, and drew the 4, giving him a 20. He is paid off at even-money. We are also paid off at even-money. It really didn't matter what totals either we or the second baseman had at this point, since the dealer busted and automatically lost. After all the discards are put away, another round of play begins. Again, we all get two cards, and the dealer's upcard this time is a J. He therefore peeks at his hole card, and when he finds he doesn't have a blackjack, he turns toward the first baseman and the game goes on as before. After a few rounds of play, even though there are cards left in the stock the dealer is holding, he'll shuffle up the cards. This is done to prevent card counters, experts who keep track of played out cards, from having an advantage over the house by

knowing what cards are left in the stock and
betting accordingly.

Multiple Deck Games

By multiple deck games, we are referring
to all games that use more than one deck.

When four or more decks are used, they're
dealt from a shoe, a rectangular box that per-
mits the cards to be slid out one at a time.

Double Deck Games

When two decks are used, these are still
hand-held and all signals used by players are
the same as in a single deck game. There are
relatively few double deck games in compari-
son with either single or four and six deck
games.

The Player's Options

Splitting Pairs

A player may split any matching cards of
the same rank (pairs) if dealt as an original
hand. For example, if he is dealt two 8s, these
may be split. When pairs are split, they are
turned over by the player if dealt face down;
or separated, if dealt face up. Then a bet equal
to the original bet is placed on the newly split
card.

For example, if a player bet $5, and received two 8s and split them, then an additional $5 bet will be placed on the separated (split) 8. In essence, the player will now be betting on and playing out two hands.

He draws cards on the first 8 till he's satisfied with that total, and then he draws cards to the second 8, just as though this was an original hand.

Any pairs can be split, and for purposes of pairs, all 10-value cards are considered pairs. For example, a 10 and Q, or J and K, are pairs, but keep in mind, 10s should not be split.

A pair of As may be split, but unlike all other pairs, only one additional card will be dealt to each A. Nevertheless, As equal 11 and they should always be split.

Doubling Down

A player may double his bet on his original hand, at his option. When he does this, he will receive an additional card, and one card only. Therefore, it's important to remember that after doubling down, you can't stand on your original hand's total; you're going to be given an additional card by the dealer.

In practically all casinos except for the Northern Nevada ones, the rules permit doubling down on any two-card total. In Northern Nevada, only 10s and 11s may be doubled down.

When doubling down, a player turns over his cards if dealt face down and puts out a bet equal to the original bet. When the cards have been dealt face up, he simply puts out an additional bet.

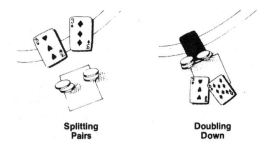

**Splitting
Pairs**

**Doubling
Down**

Surrender

In a few casinos, the player is allowed to forfeit half his original bet if he doesn't want to play the hand against the dealer. This is called surrender.

For example, suppose a player has a big bet out and the dealer shows a 10 as his upcard. The player has been dealt a 16, and feels that if he hits the hand, he'll bust, and if he stands, the dealer will have a 17 or more to beat him anyway. So, in those casinos allowing surrender, this player may surrender his hand. It's one of the few instances in which a verbal statement of the player's intent is made. He says, "Surrender," and the dealer will remove his cards and half his bet.

Insurance

When the dealer's upcard is an A, before he peeks at his hole card, the players are given the opportunity to insure their bets. The dealer will ask, "Insurance?" and the players may bet up to one-half of their original bet that the dealer has a 10-value card in the hole.

If the dealer has a blackjack, the insurance bet wins, and is paid off at 2-1, but the original bet loses. In essence, it's a standoff.

An insurance bet is really a wager that the dealer has a blackjack. If he does, the bet wins. If he doesn't have a 10-value card in the hole, the insurance bet is lost but the game continues.

For example, if a player had a $10 bet out and then made a $5 insurance bet and the dealer didn't have a blackjack, the $5 bet would be taken away by the dealer. However, the game would now continue and the original $10 bet is still valid.

If the dealer in the above instance had a blackjack, he'd take away the player's original $10 bet and then pay $10, at 2-1 on the $5 insurance bet. In essence, it's a push.

Basic Winning Strategies

Hitting and Standing Strategy

We'll divide this strategy into hard and soft totals. Remember, a hard hand is anyone that doesn't contain an A, or where an A is counted as a 1 and not an 11.

For our considerations, all hard hands will begin with a total of 12. Hands below that total can be hit without worrying about busting.

Whether to hit or stand on any hand depends on two factors: the player's total and the dealer's upcard.

The following table will show the correct hitting and standing basic strategies.

Hitting and Standing—Hard Totals									
	2	3	4	5	6	7	8	9	10	A
11/less	H	H	H	H	H	H	H	H	H	H
12	H	H	S	S	S	H	H	H	H	H
13	S	S	S	S	S	H	H	H	H	H
14	S	S	S	S	S	H	H	H	H	H
15	S	S	S	S	S	H	H	H	H	H
16	S	S	S	S	S	H	H	H	H	H
17-21	S	S	S	S	S	S	S	S	S	S

H= Hitting **S**= Standing

Whenever the dealer shows a 7 or higher upcard (8, 9, 10 or A), we assume that he already has a total of 17 and must stand with that total. Of course, that's not always the case, but it happens frequently enough for us to try and improve our total if it's below 17.

That's why we hit all hands from 12 through 16 when the dealer shows a 7, 8, 9, 10 or A.

When the dealer shows a bust or stiff card, a 2, 3, 4, 5 or 6, we stand on all totals, except a hard 12 against a dealer's 2 or 3.

The reason we hit a 12 against a dealer's 2 or 3 upcard is that there are relatively fewer cards to bust our (and the dealer's) hand in that situation. Other than a 12 against the 2 and 3, we stand on all other totals when the dealer shows a stiff card. Our strategy in this regard is to force the dealer to hit his stiff hand and bust it while we still have a valid hand.

It may be hard to memorize the table, but if you play out and practice some hands while looking at the hitting and standing table, it will become easier to understand. If you see the reasoning behind it, it's easier still.

Of course, we never hit a hard 17 or higher total, no matter what the dealer shows. The odds are strong that we'll bust. If our total is 19 or better we're favored to win by standing.

What we don't want to do is hit stiff totals from 12 to 16 when the dealer shows a 4, 5 or 6. These are the worst cards the dealer can have (and the best for us to see as upcards) because he's most likely to bust his hand with such upcards. It would be foolish of us to bust first, when the dealer has such a good chance of busting and losing.

Hitting and Standing with Soft Totals

A soft total is any hand that contains an A that is counted as 11 points. Thus, an A-6 is a soft 17. There will be two tables here—the first is to be used in all jurisdictions other than Northern Nevada, for only hard 10s and 11s can be doubled down there.

Hitting, Standing or Doubling Down with Soft Totals									
	2	3	4	5	6	7	8	9	10	A
A2-A5	H	H	D	D	D	H	H	H	H	H
A6	D	D	D	D	D	H	H	H	H	H
A7	S	D	D	D	D	S	S	H	H	S
A8	S	S	S	S	S	S	S	S	S	S
A9	S	S	S	S	S	S	S	S	S	S

H= Hitting   S= Standing   D= Double

All soft totals of 17 or below should be hit or doubled down. When the dealer shows a 4, 5 or 6 these soft totals will be doubled down.

The A-6, the soft 17, will never be stood upon. It will either be hit, or doubled down. When you see a player standing with a soft 17, you'll know he's very weak, and a loser.

The soft 19 and 20 are very strong and you should be content to stand with these totals. But the soft 18 is the tricky one. It is hit against the dealer's 9 and 10 upcard, and doubled down when the dealer holds the 3 through the 6. Practice these hands, and it will come naturally to you after a while.

The next table is for use only in Northern Nevada or any other jurisdiction where soft doubling down is not permitted.

Hitting and Standing with Soft Totals									
	2	3	4	5	6	7	8	9	10	A
A2-A6	H	H	H	H	H	H	H	H	H	H
A7	S	S	S	S	S	S	S	H	H	H
A8-A9	S	S	S	S	S	S	S	S	S	S
			H = Hit	S = Stand						

As we see from the above table, we always hit the soft 17, and hit the soft 18 against the dealer's 9 or 10. These are important rules to remember, as well as standing on soft 19 or 20.

Doubling Down Strategies

The next table shows doubling down strategies, which when correctly followed, give the player a tremendous edge over the casino. This table covers only hard doubling down totals, since the soft ones have already been covered in the previous section.

In Northern Nevada, where only a hard 10 or 11 can be doubled down, use the lines showing the 10 and 11.

Doubling Down with Hard Totals										
	2	3	4	5	6	7	8	9	10	A
8(5-3,4-4)				D	D					
9		D	D	D	D					
10	D	D	D	D	D	D	D	D		
11	D	D	D	D	D	D	D	D	D	

D = Double Down **Blank** = Don't Double Down

From this table we see that we never double down with a hard total of less than 8. Be sure to double down when you hold an 11. Many players are afraid to double down against a dealer's 10, but if you get a 10-value card on the 11, you have a 21, and can't lose.

If playing in Atlantic City, or in a casino where the dealer doesn't look at his hole card till all the players have acted upon their hands, the same double down rules apply. If the dealer finds he has a blackjack, the extra double down wager will be returned. The same holds true when splitting pairs. Only the original bet is lost.

Splitting Pairs

As we know, a player has the option of splitting any paired cards from his original hand, such as 3-3, 8-8, 9-9 and so forth. All 10-value cards are considered pairs, such as J-K, or 10-Q. The following chart shows correct splitting strategies. Split only those pairs shown on the chart.

	2	3	4	5	6	7	8	9	10	A
				Splitting Pairs						
22		spl	spl	spl	spl	spl				
33			spl	spl	spl	spl				
66	spl	spl	spl	spl	spl					
77	spl	spl	spl	spl	spl	spl				
88	spl	spl	spl	spl	spl	spl	spl	spl	spl	spl
99	spl	spl	spl	spl	spl		spl	spl		
AA	spl	spl	spl	spl	spl	spl	spl	spl	spl	spl

spl = Split   **Blank** = Don't Split
Never split 44, 55, 10s – Always split 88, AA

Be sure to split 8s and As. A pair of 8s adds up to 16, the worst stiff total a player can have, while 8s separately will form the base for a much stronger hand. As should be split, because each A adds up to 11, and a 10-value card drawn to that 11 is a powerful 21.

On the other hand, never split 4s and 5s.

Two 4s add up to 8, while an individual 4 can end up as a stiff hand and a bad one at that. The 5s together add up to 10, and in most situations will be doubled down hard. An individual 5 will usually lead to a stiff or a busted hand.

Don't split 10s (any 10-value pairs). These add up to 20, usually a winning hand. Splitting 10s is a bad move, and only the weakest players make it.

Some players will split any pair, no matter what the dealer's upcard, thinking this is correct; it isn't and will end up costing the player money. Stick to our pair splits and you'll come out a winner. They all make sense.

For example, we don't split 7s against an 8 because if the player gets two 10-value cards, one on each 7, he'll still have only 17 and the dealer might already have an 18. We don't split 9s against a dealer's 7 because two 9s add up to an 18, and the dealer might only have a 17. We split 9s against the 8 because the 18 might only be a push, whereas a 10-value card on a 9 makes it a winner.

Resplitting Pairs

If an original pair should be split, then subsequent cards of the same rank should also be split. For example, suppose the dealer shows a 6 as his upcard and you have a pair of 8s. You split the 8s and get a 5 on the first 8 for 13. Now you must stand on that hand because the Hitting and Standing Strategies call for no further cards to be drawn.

On the second 8, you're dealt another 8. This should be split and another bet put out. The rule is: resplit pairs where the fist split is correct. Not all casinos allow resplitting. For example, As generally can't be resplit. All other pairs can be resplit in practically all casinos except in Atlantic City.

Insurance

Whenever the dealer shows an A as his upcard, he'll ask if any player wants insurance. As explained before, the insurance bet is a bet that the dealer has a 10-value card in the hole and thus has a blackjack.

In most cases, it's a bad bet. Don't take insurance unless you're familiar with an advanced card counting system.

Surrender

This is allowed in some casinos, where a player may forfeit half his bet and decide not to play his or her original hand against the dealer.

When you have the chance to surrender,

stick to the following rules: surrender 15s and 16s against a dealer's 10, a 16 against a dealer's A, but make sure to not surrender 8-8, split it instead.

Otherwise, don't surrender.

Master Strategy Chart
The following chart will show you when to hit, stand, double or split, depending on what hand you have.

WINNING BLACKJACK

	Master Strategy Chart								
	2	3	4	5	6	7	8	9	10 A
7/less	H	H	H	H	H	H	H	H	H H
62	H	H	H	H	H	H	H	H	H H
44/53	H	H	H	D	D	H	H	H	H H
9	D	D	D	D	D	H	H	H	H H
10	D	D	D	D	D	D	D	D	H H
11	D	D	D	D	D	D	D	D	D D
12	H	H	S	S	S	H	H	H	H H
13	S	S	S	S	S	H	H	H	H H
14	S	S	S	S	S	H	H	H	H H
15	S	S	S	S	S	H	H	H	H H
16	S	S	S	S	S	H	H	H	H H
A2	H	H	D*	D*	D*	H	H	H	H H
A3	H	H	D*	D*	D*	H	H	H	H H
A4	H	H	D*	D*	D*	H	H	H	H H
A5	H	H	D*	D*	D*	H	H	H	H H
A6	D*	D*	D*	D*	D*	H	H	H	H H
A7	S	D*	D*	D*	D*	S	S	H	H H
A8	S	S	S	S	S	S	S	S	S S
A9	S	S	S	S	S	S	S	S	S S
22	H	spl	spl	spl	spl	spl	H	H	H H
33	H	H	spl	spl	spl	spl	H	H	H H
66	spl	spl	spl	spl	spl	H	H	H	H H
77	spl	spl	spl	spl	spl	spl	H	H	H H
88	spl	spl	spl	spl	spl	spl	spl	spl	spl spl
99	spl	spl	spl	spl	spl	S	spl	spl	S S
AA	spl	spl	spl	spl	spl	spl	spl	spl	spl spl

H= Hit   **S**= Stand   **D**= Double   **spl** = Split

Where soft doubling is not permitted, hit instead

Card Counting and Money Management

Card Counting

Card counting, or keeping track of the cards already played out, is used by experts to beat the casino, and many of these experts have been barred from play.

This guidebook is not going to deal with card counting, other than to state that when a high proportion of 10-value cards and As have been dealt out, the deck is unfavorable for the player. On the other hand, when many smaller cards, such as 2s–7s have been dealt out, the deck or decks are favorable for the player.

By watching the game closely, a player can get a good idea of the cards already dealt. For example, if on the first round of play in a single deck game, a disproportionate number of As and 10s were dealt, then the deck is unfavorable. If a whole group of smaller cards showed on the opening round, with few As or 10s, then the deck is favorable.

A good rule in a single deck game is to raise the bet when the first round showed a high proportion of small cards dealt out, and to lower the bet when this round showed a higher proportion of 10s and As.

With each round that follows, you see that

cumulatively, more 10s than normal have been dealt, keep your bet low. But, when you notice more small cards have been played, raise your bet. This works because a single deck is sensitive to changes in deck composition.

To effectively beat the casinos, either at single or multi-deck games, we recommend that you learn a card counting strategy.

See back for information on the GRI Pro-Count, the most effective card counting strategy ever produced for the average player. It's simple to learn yet very powerful. It will give any reader of this book a winning edge over the casino with just a few hours practice.

Money Management

Blackjack games can be like roller coasters, with large winning and losing swings during the course of play. Be prepared and don't get discouraged because correct play will make you a winner in the long run.

As a rule of thumb, multiply your bet by 40 to determine how much to put on the table for one session of play. If you're betting $2 at a time, $80 will be sufficient. With $5 bets, about $200 will be needed. You can even hedge and take less, about $50 for $2 bets and $100 for $5 bets, but that's cutting it a little too thin.

Remember, play only with money you can

afford to lose. Try to double your stake at the table. If you do, leave at once. You've done well. Or, if the table is choppy, and you're ahead, endeavor to leave a winner.

If you're losing, don't lose more than you bring to the table. Set a loss limit, and never reach into your pocket for money. The first loss is the cheapest.

Money management can be as important as good play. Keep control of your emotions and your money and you'll be a winner.

Glossary of Blackjack Terms

Anchorman—Also called **Third Baseman**. The player in the last seat or the player who acts upon his hand last at the table.

Blackjack—(1.) The casino game; also called "21." (2.) An original hand consisting of an A and 10-value card, paid off at 3-2 if held by a player.

Burning a Card—The removal of the top card by the dealer before dealing out cards on the first round of play.

Breaking—Also known as **Busting**. Drawing cards to a hand so that its total is 22 or more, a loser.

Busting—See **Breaking**.

Card Counting—Keeping mental track of

the cards played out to see if the deck is favorable or unfavorable.

Chips—The gambling tokens issued by the casino to take the place of cash, for betting purposes.

Dealer—The casino employee in charge of the blackjack game, who deals out cards and collects and pays off bets.

Deck—The standard pack of cards containing 52 cards of four suits.

Double Down—The doubling of an original bet by a player, who will then receive only one additional card.

Draw—The act of getting one or more cards for the original hand. Also called **Hit**.

Favorable Deck—A deck whose remaining cards are to the advantage of the player as far as probability of winning is concerned.

First Baseman—The player who receives cards and acts upon them first. Usually occupies the first end seat at the table.

Hand—Cards the players hold and act upon.

Hit—See **Draw**.

Hole Card—The unseen dealer's card.

Insurance—A bet that can be made when a dealer shows an A as an upcard. This bet wins if the dealer has a blackjack.

Multiple Deck—The use of more than one deck in the game of casino blackjack.

Natural—Another term for a blackjack.

Push—A tie between the dealer and player–no money changes hands. It's a standoff.

Round of Play—A complete cycle of play where all the players and the dealer act upon their hands.

Shoe—A device used when dealing four or more decks.

Shuffle, Shuffle Up—The mixing up of the cards by the dealer.

Single Deck Game—A game in which only one deck of cards is used.

Soft Total—A hand containing an A that counts as 11 points. Example, an A-9 is a soft 20 total.

Splitting Pairs—The separation of two cards of equal rank, such as 8s, so that they're played as two separate hands.

Standing, Standing Pat—Not hitting a hand.

Stiff Hand—Any hand that may bust if drawn to, such as a hard 12-16.

Ten-Value Card—The 10, J, Q or K, all valued at ten points.

Tip or Toke—A gratuity given to or bet for the dealer by the player.

Twenty-One—Another name for blackjack.

Upcard—The open card of the dealer which can be seen by the player prior to their acting on their hands.

Winning Craps

Introduction

Craps is certainly the most exciting and fastest of all casino games. There's action on every roll of the dice. It's also a game in which one can let loose; it doesn't matter how excited you get at the table, or how you show your emotions. Although this makes the game exciting and fun, it's still a casino game, and money can be won or lost while playing it. This chapter shows you how to play the game correctly, how to make the best bets, and how to come out a winner if luck is on your side.

We'll review each aspect of the game, so that even the novice craps player will know all that is necessary to play the game intelligently and avoid the worst bets, the ones that favor the house with too much of an edge.

Following the advice outlined in this chapter will give you the best chance of winning at this most exciting of games. Good luck.

Understanding the Dice

The game of casino craps is played with two **dice**. Each **die** has six numbered sides.

The numbers are in the form of dots, running from one to six. Thus, with two dice in play, the lowest number that can be rolled is 2, made up of the one spot coming up on each die. The highest number is 12, made up of six spots coming up on each die. With two dice in operation, there are thirty-six possible combinations that can be rolled, with the numbers from 2 to 12 as possibilities.

Casino dice are built to exacting standards, so that there is little chance of certain numbers showing up more often than others because of faulty design or manufacture. They're approximately 3/4 of an inch measured on each side, and are made as close to exact cubes as modern machinery will allow.

When you're playing the game, and it's your turn to roll the dice, if you look closely, you'll see imprinted on the dice two other things besides the dots representing the numbers. First of all, you'll see the name of the casino, or its logo. There will also be a code number. Individual sets of dice are made for particular casinos, often in a particular color, such as green or red, which are the most common in American gambling casinos. In addition, code numbers are put on the dice so that cheats can't substitute other dice for the ones regularly used. This safeguards both the casino and the players in the course of a game.

Dice Combinations

The next table shows all the possible combinations of two rolled dice.

The 7 can be rolled no matter what number shows up on one die; it is unique in that respect. For example, a 6 cannot be rolled if a 6 shows up on one die, and an 8 can't be rolled if a 1 shows up on any die.

The 7 is the most important number by far in the game of casino craps, and determines all the odds.

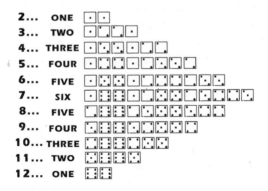

2...	ONE	
3...	TWO	
4...	THREE	
5...	FOUR	
6...	FIVE	
7...	SIX	
8...	FIVE	
9...	FOUR	
10...	THREE	
11...	TWO	
12...	ONE	

Correct Odds, House Payoff and Edge

The **house advantage,** or **edge,** is the difference between the player's chances of winning the bet, called the **correct odds**, and the casino's actual payoff, called the **house payoff** or simply, the **payoff**. For example, the correct odds of rolling a 7 are 5 to 1. Since the house will payoff only 4 to 1 should the 7 be thrown, they maintain an edge of 16.67 percent on this wager.

The Table and Layout

The Table

The average craps table is about the size of a large billiards table and is built to accommodate anywhere from twelve to twenty-four players. There is a felt covered surface known as the **layout**, around which are walls which form the table, and on which are rails to hold the players' chips.

The main purpose of the layout is to give the players what they're at the casino for—action. They have a chance to make a variety of bets, all of which are favorable to the house (that is, the odds on each bet favor the house).

We can see that there are essentially three sections on the layout.

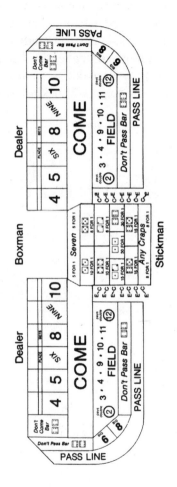

There are two identical side areas separated by a center area. The center area is where all the center, or proposition, bets are made. As we shall see, none of the bets in this section are worth a red penny; they're all bad, that is, highly unfavorable to the player. The following is the center layout.

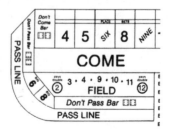

The two side areas are identical and they contain the best wagers for the player to make, since they give the house the smallest advantage over the gamblers. This is the best area to put your money.

Casino Personnel

The Crew of Dealers

A casino craps crew is made up of four individuals, but only three work the table at one time, with the fourth on break, that is, taking a rest from his chores. The crew usually is made up of men, though more and more women are seen as integral parts of craps crews.

The men and women who make up the working crew do not have set jobs at the table. They move around from position to position. This rotation keeps them alert and adds flavor to the game, for each dealer has a different personality and an upbeat dealer or crew can make a game come alive.

The Stickman

One of the dealers faces the other two. He is known as the **stickman**, or is said to be **on the stick**. He has this title because he holds a soft-tipped stick in his hand, which is used, first of all, to push the dice to a new shooter, then to gather in dice that have been thrown and hold them till all payoffs and collections have been made by the other dealers.

The stickman is also in charge of all the center or **proposition bets**, which are under his direct control. He collects losing bets and pushes them to the boxman, whom we will discuss later. The stickman directs the other dealers to pay off winning bets that occur on the center of the table.

If a player makes a proposition or center bet, the chips are thrown to the stickman to be put in the correct betting box. The stickman doesn't pay off bets, though, and he has no direct contact with the players except for pushing the dice toward the shooter with his stick.

The dealer on the stick has one other important duty. He calls the game. If a new shooter is to be selected, he announces *"New shooter coming out."* If there is a come-out roll, he announces that as well. After the dice are thrown, he calls the number thrown, such as *"Five."* He may also add, *"Five, no field,"* to indicate that it is not paid off on the field bets.

Often the personality of the stickman infuses the craps game and determines whether it will be lively or dull.

Dealers On-Base

These are the two standing dealers who face the stickman, and each covers an end area of the layout. They have direct contact with the players. They make change, **change color**

WINNING CRAPS

(change chips for others of different denominations), pay off winning bets, and collect losing ones.

They also handle the players' chips when players want to make center bets or bets they can't reach, such as odds bets on don't come and come points.

These dealers are said to be **on base**. When you first come to a table, you'll give your cash to a dealer on base. He'll give you the correct casino chips as soon as the sum is verified by the boxman.

The standing dealer will also answer any questions you might have about the table limits, how much you can wager on any particular bet, and whether single or double odds are permitted at the table.

Each standing dealer has a **marker puck**, a black and white round plastic disk, which is on its black side in the corner don't come box prior to a come-out roll. This disk is turned to its white side and put into a point number box after a point is established on the **come-out roll**. A come-out roll will be explained later.

First and foremost, the dealer is there to help you, the player, to make certain your bets have been correctly made and to answer any of your questions about the game.

The Boxman

The crew of dealers wear the house uniform, but the boxman is usually dressed in a jacket or suit. He is in charge of the game, and sits between the two on-base dealers, facing the stickman.

The boxman supervises the game, makes sure that the payoffs are correct, makes certain that the cash given to the dealer is verified, and, in short, protects the casino's bankroll, for most of the chips on the table are right in front of him, under his domain and protection.

If the dice are thrown off the table, they must first be returned to the boxman, who examines the die or dice to make sure they haven't been tampered with and are the same die or dice that were thrown, and not new dice inserted in the game by cheats. To do this, he looks for both the casino logo and the coded number on all casino dice.

If there's a dispute between a player and a dealer, as sometimes happens, the boxman has the final word. Generally, he will side with the player, unless it is a flagrant objection by the player, but thereafter, in further disputes, he won't give the player the benefit of the doubt.

WINNING CRAPS

Casino Executives

Since craps table revenue is an important aspect of the profits of a casino, not only are the crew of dealers and boxman involved with the game, but behind the table, in the *craps pit*, are several other casino employees, executives of the house. These might include a **floorman**, who supervises a couple of tables, and is there in case any of the players want to get credit. Above him, in charge of all the craps tables in what is known as the craps pit, is the pitboss, the final authority on credit and disputes.

Tipping

Tipping, or **toking**, as it is called in the casinos, is a voluntary practice. Only the crew of dealers are tipped, not the boxman or the casino executives. If a player is winning a lot and feels in a buoyant mood, or if he has received good services from the dealers, then he may tip them. The usual practice is to make a bet *for the boys* by throwing a chip toward the center or proposition bets, and making one of those high yielding but poor odds bets. Just say "*For the boys*." The crew will understand that this bet is for them, and should thank you for it. They appreciate tokes because that's their main source of their income.

How to Play Craps

In this section, we're not just going to study how to play craps, we'll also show the essential game, what's involved, and so forth. So let's imagine that you know nothing about the game, and you're in a gambling casino, approaching a craps table. There are a few open spots around the rails and you move into one of them.

The first thing you want to do is make a bet, but before you can do that, we should change your cash into casino chips, or **checks,** as the professionals call them. You can play with cash, make bets in cash all night long, but the casino discourages this, for it's cumbersome and slows the game down, as it has to be counted and recounted. Chips are easier, fit into betting areas better, and can be paid off more easily. In fact, even if you wager in cash, you'll be paid off with chips.

Casino Chips

Chips usually come in standard denominations of $1, $5, $25 and $100. Some casinos have $500 or larger denomination chips and others have smaller denominations, down to 25¢ chips. For purposes of this book we're going to stick with the $1 to $100 chips.

All right, you're at the table, and you take some cash out of your pocket. You're going to gamble with $200 worth. Give the cash to the standing dealer nearest you, and the cash will go over to the seated boxman who'll count and verify its amount. Once it's verified, he'll tell the dealer to give you $200 in chips, while the cash is pushed down with a paddle into a slot on the table, to fall into a **drop box**.

Now the casino has your cash, but you have its chips. The dealer will ask what denominations you want. You might ask for a stack of twenty $5 chips and four $25 chips. Long-time gamblers refer to $5 chips as **nickels** and $25 chips as **quarters**. The dealer will hand you twenty $5 chips and four $25 chips and now you're ready to make a bet.

The Shooter

When you arrive at the table, someone will be ready to throw the dice. This is the **shooter**. Whatever he throws is what determines whether bets are won or lost.

Let's assume that a new shooter is about to be given the dice. Each player gets a turn at being a shooter. The dice go around the table in a clockwise manner. Anyone who's selected as the shooter may pass up the chance; there's no stigma attached to not being a shooter. If the dice are refused, then the next person to that player's left will be offered the dice.

The shooter will be given from six to eight dice, of which he'll select only two. He will generally roll with these same dice for his entire shoot, though sometimes eccentric players will change the dice, or if one is rolled off the table or temporarily lost, another one will replace the lost die.

This decision rests solely with the shooter. Other players at the table can't demand that the dice be changed. While a person is a shooter, he or she is the center of attention.

The Line and Free-Odds Bets

Making A Bet

Before the shooter rolls the dice for the first time, or after he has made his point (which will be explained later) there is a *come-out* roll. Prior to the come-out roll, most of the players at the table bet either for or against the dice by making either a pass-line or a don't pass bet. This is done by putting a chip or chips into the appropriate areas on the layout. By far the most popular bet in casino craps is the pass-line wager.

Pass-Line Wager and Come-Out Roll

The area that accommodates the pass-line bet runs the full length of each side area, to give the bettors easy access to this wager.

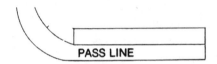

This bet can be made only prior to the opening roll of the dice, the come-out roll. A come-out roll can easily be ascertained, for there is a round disk that is black and white and when it is resting on its black side in the corner of the numbered boxes, in the don't come box, then there is a come-out roll about to commence.

When this same disk is on its white side and in one of the numbered boxes on the lay-out, in the 4, 5, 6, 8, 9 or 10 box, then that is the point established by the come-out roll, and no more line bets are permitted. A **line bet** is either a pass-line or don't pass wager.

The come-out roll is the most important throw in craps. It determines either immediate wins or losses, or what point is established.

The bettor wagering on the pass-line wants the dice to win, or pass. He is known as the right bettor, and wins immediately at even-money if:

A 7 or 11 is rolled on the come-out.

He loses immediately if:

A 2, 3 or 12— known as craps—is rolled on the come-out.

When a shooter rolls a 2, 3 or 12, he is said to have crapped out, but he doesn't lose his shoot. After all pass-line bets are collected, and all don't pass bets paid off, he continues his shoot.

If the come-out roll is a 4, 5, 6, 8, 9 or 10, that number is the point, and must be repeated before a 7 is thrown for the pass-line bet to win. All other numbers are immaterial to this result, once a point has been established on the come-out. For example, if the point is 4, and subsequently an 11, 12, 3, 2, 8, 8, 9 and 4 are rolled, the pass-line bet is won, because the 4 repeated before a 7 was thrown. None of the other numbers rolled mattered as to this result.

Don't Pass Bet

A player betting **don't pass** is betting

against the dice, wagering that they don't pass, or win. He is known as a **wrong** bettor, and he places his chip or chips in the smaller area reserved for don't pass.

A don't pass bettor wins immediately at even-money if:

A 2 or 3 is rolled on the come-out.

He loses immediately if:

A 7 or 11 is rolled.

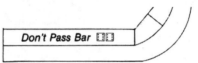

If a 12 is rolled, there's a standoff, and he neither wins nor loses. In some gambling jurisdictions the 2 is substituted for the 12, with the same effect. The 12 or 2 is **barred**, permitting the casino to keep its edge on don't pass wagers.

If a point number is established, the don't pass bettor wins if a 7 comes up before the point is repeated. He loses if the point is repeated before a 7 comes up. The house edge on all line bets, whether they be pass-line or don't pass, is 1.4%. When a player makes these bets, he is giving the house or casino a theoretical win expectation of $1.40 for each $100 bet. He can reduce this house edge substantially, however, by making another bet at the same time he makes the line bet. This additional wager is not shown on the layout, but it is permissible, and all intelligent craps players should make it. It's known as the free-odds bet.

The Free-Odds Bet

This bet can only be made *after* a point number has been established on the come-out. It's made by putting additional chips behind the original bet for pass-line bettors. If won, this additional wager will be paid off at true and correct odds, giving the casino no advantage whatsoever on the wager. That's why it's known as a free-odds bet. If the point is a 4 or 10, the free-odds bet will be paid off at 2-1; a 5 or 9 will be paid off at 3-2, and a 6 or 8 will be paid off at 6-5.

Odds of Point Repeating Before Seven		
Point Number	Correct Odds	House Payoff
4 or 10	2 to 1	2 to 1
5 or 9	3 to 2	3 to 2
6 or 8	6 to 5	6 to 5

In most casinos the player is limited to a free-odds bet equal to his original pass-line bet. In those casinos the bet is then called a

single odds bet. The good news is that, even if one is limited to single odds, a bettor can wager a little more behind the line in certain instances.

For example, if a player bet $5 on the pass-line and the point is 5 or 9, then he's permitted to wager $6 as a free odds bet because the payoff is 3-2, and most casinos won't pay off in half-dollar increments.

When the point is 4 or 10, no matter what is bet, the same amount must be wagered as a free odds bet since the payoff is 2-1.

If the point is 6 and 8, though, most casinos will permit a $5 free odds bet if the player bets at least $3 on the pass-line. Unless $5 is bet behind the line, the payoff on the odds bet won't be the correct 6-5, because the house doesn't pay off in half-dollars. For example, if a gambler bet $6 on the pass-line, and then $6 on the free odds bet if the point was 8, the free odds payoff would be $7, which represents $6 for the first $5 bet, and only $1 at even-money for the extra dollar bet. In order to get the correct free odds return, when the point is 6 or 8, the bets behind the line must be in increments of $5. When the point is 5 or 9, the free odds bet must be in increments of $2.

What happens when a pass-line bet and free-odds bet win? What's the payoff? Let's assume a player bets $10 on the pass-line and a point is established. He then puts $10 behind the line as a free-odds bet. Here are the payoffs:

Single Odds Payoffs: Right Bettors			
Point	Pass-Line Payoff	Free-Odds Payoff	Total
4 or 10	$10	$20 (2-1)	$30
5 or 9	$10	$15 (3-2)	$25
6 or 8	$10	$12 (6-5)	$22

If the 7 comes up before the point is repeated, then the player loses both the pass-line and free-odds bets.

When making a free-odds bet, the player reduces the overall house edge from 1.4% to 0.8%, a substantial reduction.

In some casinos, players are permitted to make **double odds** bets. In these casinos, the bettor can place *twice his original bet* behind the line as a free-odds bet. Thus, if he bet $10 on the pass-line, he can put $20 behind the line at correct payoffs. Here's what these payoffs would look like with a $10 pass-line and $20 free-odds bet.

Double Odds Payoffs: Right Bettors			
Point	**Pass-Line Payoff**	**Free-Odds Payoff**	**Total**
4 or 10	$10	$40 (2-1)	$50
5 or 9	$10	$30 (3-2)	$40
6 or 8	$10	$24 (6-5)	$34

A double free-odds bet reduces the house edge down to 0.6%.

Free-odds wagers can be made at any time after a point is established, and can be removed at the player's option at any time prior to a seven-out or the point's being repeated. Since it's to a player's advantage to make a free-odds bet, he or she should always make it, and it should never be removed.

Don't Pass—Laying Free-Odds

A gambler who bets don't pass, hoping that the 7 will come up before the point is repeated, can also make free-odds bets. Whereas the pass-line bettor is taking odds, the don't pass bettor is **laying odds**. By making this advantageous bet, the player reduces the casino's overall edge from 1.4% to 0.8%

Odds of Rolling Seven Before Point Repeats		
Point Number	**Correct Odds**	**House Payoff**
4 or 10	1 to 2	1 to 2
5 or 9	2 to 3	2 to 3
6 or 8	5 to 6	5 to 6

For example, if a don't pass bettor had put down $10 in the don't pass area and the come-out roll was a 5, then 5 is the point. Now this same don't pass gambler can bet $15 as a free-odds bet. What he is doing is betting $15 to win $10, since he is laying 3-2 against the 5's being made. Should the shooter seven-out and not repeat the point, then the don't pass player would win $10 for his don't pass bet and an additional $10 for his free odds bet.

When single odds are permitted, they are determined by the *payoff* amount, not the amount that can be laid against the point. Thus, if the line bet is $10 and the point is 4 or 10, a $20 free-odds bet laid against these points will yield a payoff of $10. Likewise $15 against a 5 or 9 will give a payoff of $10, and with a 6 or 8 as the point, the payoff will be $10 if $12 is laid. The following table shows the payoffs if $10 is bet on don't pass and single odds are laid against the various points.

Single Odds Payoffs: Wrong Bettors			
Point	Don't Pass Payoff	Free-Odds Payoff	Total
4 or 10	$10	$10 ($20-$10)	$20
5 or 9	$10	$10 ($15-$10)	$20
6 or 8	$10	$10 ($12-$10)	$20
6 or 8	$10	$10 ($12-$10)	$20

Like other free-odds bets, these may be laid or taken off at any time after a point is established, at the option of the player.

Some casinos allow double odds bets, and in those houses, a player may lay double the amount he can in a single odds casino. Again, the payoff, not the amount of the odds bet, determines how much may be laid.

Thus, a gambler betting $10 as a don't pass bet can lay $40 ($40-$20) if the point is 4 or 10, $30 ($30-$20) if the point is 5 or 9, and $24 ($24-$20) if the point is 6 or 8. When double odds are laid, the house edge is reduced 0.6%.

Of course, if the point is made, the don't pass player loses both his original don't pass bet and his single or double free-odds bet.

These bets tend to be a little difficult for most players to figure out, but they're really not hard to understand. Since they offer the best odds on the table, along with the line bets, a craps player should certainly be conversant with them and use them to his or her advantage.

Come and Don't Come Bets

Come Bets

A large section of the layout is devoted to

come bets.

COME

This bet is the same as a pass-line bet, with just one difference: it can be made only *after* the come-out roll. Let's assume that on the come-out roll, the number thrown was a 9. Now 9 is the point number. At this time, any player can make a come bet.

The come bet is made by putting a chip or chips into the come box. On the very next roll of the dice, if the number is 7 or 11, the come bet wins at even-money. If it's a 2, 3 or 12, the come bet loses immediately. If any other number is rolled, a 4, 5, 6, 8, 9 or 10, then that's the come point. The chips are moved by the dealer to the appropriate number box, which also houses the place bets (discussed later).

The player may make a free-odds bet on the come point just as he could on the pass-line point. If the table is single odds, then the player should give the dealer a bet equal to the come bet and tell him "odds." The dealer will place the chip or chips at a slight tilt on the come bet in the appropriate box number. If this casino plays double odds, then the player can hand the dealer an odds bet double the original come bet.

Let's assume, after the come-out roll of 9, that the next number is 10, and a player had bet $5 on the come. This $5 is moved to box 10, and the player gives the dealer an additional $5 as a free-odds bet. As to the come bet, all that concerns this player is whether a 10 repeats before the 7. All other numbers are immaterial to the outcome of this bet. If a 10 repeats, the player will be paid $5 for the come bet, and $10 for the free-odds bet at 2-1.

If a 7 comes up before the 10 repeats, then the player loses both the come and free-odds bets.

Let's assume that instead of a 10 being thrown on the first roll after the come-out, a 7 was rolled. This is an immediate winner for the come bet even though it loses the pass-line bet. Each come roll must be treated as a bet separate from a pass-line wager.

Now, after that 7 is rolled, a player can't make another come bet because there's a new come-out roll, and come bets can be made only after a come-out roll, not at the same time.

Other than timing, the only difference between a pass-line bet and a come bet is that, if a 7 is thrown on the come-out roll and the player has one or more come bets working, he loses the underlying come bets (because a 7 came up before these numbers were repeated) but he doesn't lose the free-odds bets.

On the come-out roll, the free-odds bets on come wagers aren't *working*. That is, they're **off**. Thus if a player had come bets of $10 each on the 5 and 6, and also had $10 free-odds on each of those come points, and a 7 was rolled on the come-out roll, he'd lose only $20 on the underlying bets. The $20 in free-odds bets would be returned to him.

Conversely, if either the 5 or 6 had been thrown on the come-out roll, the player would be paid only $10 for the number's repeating, and wouldn't get the additional odds bet as a winner. It would simply be returned to him.

Why make come bets? They give the house the same low percentage that it gets on pass-line bets. They also enable the player to make a whole series of consecutive wagers at good odds, so if the dice get *hot* and a lot of numbers are rolled before a 7 comes up, he can really make a lot of money in a short period of time. But remember that when that 7 shows, all the come bets are lost, erased from the table.

Don't Come Bets

The don't come box is much smaller than the come box on the layout, usually tucked in at the end of the place number boxes.

Don't Come Bar			PLACE	BETS		
⊞⊞	4	5	SIX	8	NINE	10

There's usually not that much action on don't come, but that doesn't mean it isn't a valid bet. It's the same as a don't pass bet except for timing, and after the bet is made a player can lay odds against the number just as he or she can on a don't pass bet. The house edge is the same as a don't pass bet, 0.8% when single odds are laid and 0.6% when double odds are laid.

After a come point is rolled, the chip or chips will be taken from the don't come box by the dealer and placed in the area above the numbered box of that come point. The player must give the dealer additional chips to lay odds against the number's repeating.

On a don't come bet, if a 7 or 11 is rolled, it's an immediate loser for the don't come player. If a 2 or 3 is rolled, it's an immediate winner at even-money, and if a 12 is rolled, it's a standoff. The same as don't pass in all respects except for timing.

Unlike come bets, don't come bets and odds are always working, even on the come-out roll, so that the player's underlying don't come bets and odds bets are always at risk.

On the other hand, if a 7 comes up on the come-out roll, then all the don't come bets are winners, including the free-odds bets laid against the numbers.

Why make don't come bets? The player is hoping for a cold run of dice, where no numbers are repeated. So, after several don't come bets are established, he hopes a 7 comes up and wins all the bets for him. Of course, if a lot of numbers repeat, then he'll be losing those same bets. But the house edge is very small and on a cold table, don't come bets are a good way to make money fast.

Free-Odds Bet: Come & Don't Come

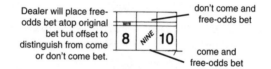

Dealer will place free-odds bet atop original bet but offset to distinguish from come or don't come bet.

don't come and free-odds bet

come and free-odds bet

Place Numbers and Place Bets

The area where place bets can be made is rather large, for not only do place bets get a lot of action, but the same area also holds the come and don't come bets.

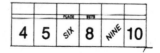

WINNING CRAPS

Place bets can be made on one or more of the numbers that are point numbers: 4, 5, 6, 8, 9 and 10. A place bet can be made at any time, even prior to a come-out roll, but place bets are off and not working on the come-out roll, unless the player wishes them to be working and so instructs the dealer.

Place bets can be made in any denomination up to the house limit, which is generally $500 on all numbers but the 6 and 8, which have $600 limits. Because of the payoffs, place bets should be made in increments of $5 for all numbers but the 6 and 8, for which they should be in increments of $6. Like come bets, place bets are favored by players betting *right*, or with the dice. Also like come bets, place bets promote action on every roll of the dice. Unlike come bets, a place bet doesn't have to repeat twice for the bettor to receive a payoff. Once a bettor makes a place bet, he's paid off as soon as that number is rolled.

To get this kind of action, the gambler pays a price. It comes in the form of the house edge, which is much higher on place bets than on come bets.

CARDOZA PUBLISHING • ALLEN

| Place Number | Odds on Place Numbers | | Casino Edge |
	Casino Payoff	Correct Odds	
4 or 10	9-5	2-1	6.67%
5 or 9	7-5	3-2	4.0%
6 or 8	7-6	6-5	1.52%

As we can easily see, the only possible worthwhile place bet is on the 6 and 8; otherwise the house edge is just too much.

Not only can a player make place bets at any time, but he can also raise, lower or remove them at any time. To change your place bets, just hand chips to the dealer or instruct him to remove your chips.

Why make place bets? There's really no reason to do so, unless you're betting on the 6 and 8. If there's a long, hot roll, with many numbers repeating, the payoffs can be tremendous. The house edge is horrendous, though, and will usually eat up your bankroll before you reap the benefit of those long rolls.

Buying the 4 and 10

The house edge on the 4 and 10 can be reduced to 4.73% by **buying** either or both numbers. You make this bet by instructing the dealer that you are *"buying"* the 4 or 10 or both numbers, and then handing him the correct number of chips. A buy button will then

84

be put on those chips. The payoff will be 2-1, but each time you get paid off, you pay the equivalent of a 5% commission. In most casinos this commission must be paid at the time the numbers are bought.

Either buying or placing the 4 and 10 is not recommended because of the large house edge.

Lay Wagers

Players who bet against the dice can lay bets against any of the point numbers by instructing the dealers that they are *laying* against one or more of these numbers. A 5% commission must be paid at this time. This gives the casino the following edges:

House Edge on Lay Wager	
Number	Casino Edge
4 or 10	2.44%
5 or 9	3.23%
6 or 8	4.0%

As with place bets, chips for lay wagers are given to the dealer. A player can make, reduce, or take off these bets at any time, in any combinations.

Other Bets

Field Bets

These bets are a favorite of beginners or ignorant players. They're easy to make, can be made at any time on any roll of the dice, and are paid off or lost immediately. There's a price to pay, though, and that's a high casino edge.

The field bet takes up a prominent place on the casino layout.

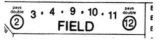

All those numbers look inviting. The 3, 4, 9, 10 and 11 all pay at even-money. The 2 and 12 vary depending upon the casino. In places where they pay at 2-1, such as on the Strip, the house edge on a field bet is 5.5%. In Atlantic City, Northern Nevada and Downtown Las Vegas, where either the 2 or the 12 is paid at 3-1, the house edge drops to 2.7%.

In either case, a field bet is not the best kind of wager to make. The numbers that are missing from the field—the 5, 6, 7 and 8—come up more ways than the numbers on the field layout. Though the field looks inviting, and a bet there is quick and easy to make, the odds of your winning are rather dismal. Avoid the field.

Big Six and Big Eight

This bet is prominently displayed, but only small timers make it, putting down a dollar or two and hoping that the 6 or 8 will come up before the 7 is rolled, so that they can collect their even-money winnings.

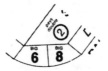

But there are only five ways to roll a 6 and five ways to roll an 8, and there are six ways to roll a 7. So the true odds against making the 6 or 8 are 6-5, and when the casino pays off at even-money, it has a 9.09% edge. A player should never make this bet except in certain Atlantic City casinos, which will pay off the Big 6 and Big 8 at 7-6, the same as a 6 or 8 place bet, if the bettor puts at least $6 or increments of $6 in the Big 6 or Big 8 box. In places that pay only even-money, avoid this bet.

Proposition or Center Bets

These bets take up the whole center of the layout and are under the control of the stickman. A good player should never make any of these bets, since the house edge on them is huge.

Though the stickman will physically handle the placing and removing of bets in this area, the player will generally make his bets and receive his payoffs through the dealer.

The center bets can be divided into one-roll and other proposition bets.

One Roll Bets

A One-Roll wager wins or loses depending only on the very next throw of the dice. The following table shows the true odds against rolling any of these numbers. Since there are thirty-six possible combinations, the odds are figured by dividing the number of ways to roll any particular number into 36.

Odds of One Roll Bets		
Number	**Ways to Roll**	**Odds Against on Single Roll**
2 or 12	1	35-1
3 or 11	2	17-1
7	6	5-1

Any 7

Any 7 pays off at 4 to 1, whereas the true odds are 5-1 against a 7's being rolled on the next roll, giving the house a 16.67% edge. Sometimes the bet is paid off at "5 for 1," which is the same as 4-1. When you see "for" between odds numbers, reduce the first number by one. So 5 for 1 means 4-1.

Any Craps

The true odds against rolling either a 2, 3, or 12 on a single roll are 8-1, but the casino pays only 7-1, which gives it an 11.1% edge.

The 2 or 12

If you bet that the next roll of the dice will be a 2, the odds are 35-1 against your winning. The same odds apply to a 12, since there is only one way to roll either number. The casino pays only 30-1 on these wagers, giving it an advantage of 13.89%.

The 3 or 11

The true odds against rolling a 3 on the next throw of the dice are 17-1. The same odds apply to the 11, since either can be rolled in only two ways. The house pays off on these bets at only 15-1, which gives it an advantage of 11.1%.

Horn Bet

This bet is often seen in Atlantic City or Northern Nevada. It requires four chips placed on the 2, 3, 11 and 12. Since the casino pays off at its usual bad odds if any one of these is rolled, you're getting four bad bets at once. Don't make a horn bet.

Other Proposition Bets: The Hardways

A **hardway** is the number 4 coming up as 2-2, the number 6 coming up as 3-3, the number 8 coming up as 4-4, or the number 10 coming up as 5-5. In other words, these four numbers are said to have come up "hard" if identical spots show on each die.

These aren't one-roll bets. When a player bets on a hardway number, he is wagering that the number will come up hard rather than easy, and before a 7 is rolled.

If a 4 is rolled as a 1-3, 6 is rolled as a 1-5 or 2-4, 8 is rolled as a 2-6 or 3-5, or 10 is rolled as a 4-6, that's an **easy** number. Remember, the easy ways and the 7 defeat a hardway bet.

Hard 4 and Hard 10

The true odds on these bets are 8-1, but the casino pays off at 7-1, giving it an 11.1% edge. Don't make the bet.

Hard 6 and Hard 8

The true odds on these bets are 10-1, but the casino will only pay 9-1, giving it an edge of 9.09%. This bet should never be made.

Winning Craps Play

There are two ways to approach a craps table. One is to bet with the dice, hoping they'll pass, that numbers will repeat, and that the come-out roll will feature a lot of 7s and 11s. A bettor who wants the dice to pass is known as a right bettor. The term does not have any moral implications. It simply designates a player betting with the dice.

A player who doesn't want the dice to pass, who bets don't pass, is looking for a lot of craps—2s and 3s—on the come-out and a lot of 7s after a point is established. This bettor is wagering against the dice and is known as a wrong bettor.

The odds are roughly the same whether

you bet right or wrong. You have an equal chance of winning, but remember, casino craps is a negative game, and only correct and smart play (coupled with some luck) will make you a winner. If you make foolish bets, bets in which the house has a big edge over you, there's hardly any chance you'll walk away a winner from a casino craps table.

Right Bettors—Correct Play

A right player should make only bets which give the house its minimum edge. The best and most conservative method of play is to make a pass-line wager, and, if a point is established, to take the maximum odds allowed on that point. If you're uncertain about how much you can wager as an odds bet, ask the dealer.

If a player wants a little more action, he can also make a come bet or two come bets, and again take the maximum free-odds.

Betting this way, a player can win a bit of money on a lucky or hot roll, and he's meanwhile giving the house only 0.8% in a single odds game and 0.6% in a double odds game.

This kind of gambler will be known as a *tough* player, because he's making only the best bets, giving the house very little in the way of an edge. If lady luck smiles upon him, he can make a good bit of change with this method.

A more aggressive bettor, after making a pass-line and one or two come bets, all with maximum free-odds, can then also make place wagers on the 6 or 8 if they're not already bet. Although this player is now giving the casino a bigger edge (1.52%), as long as the dice pass and some long rolls develop, the gambler can make a lot of money.

Don't under any circumstances make any other bet, no matter how tempting the payoffs may be. The house edge is just too great, and will wear down your bankroll in no time. Craps is a fast game. The play moves fast, and you can also lose your money fast. So be careful and bet wisely.

Wrong Bettors—Correct Play

The wrong bettor should make a don't pass bet and then lay *single* odds against the point. Even though double odds will slightly reduce the house edge from 0.8% to 0.6%, a series of repeated points will quickly make the bets disappear, along with the player's bankroll.

The wrong bettor should also make one, and, if he's more aggressive, two don't come wagers. Last, he can lay single odds against the come wagers, and stop.

Those are the only bets a wrong bettor should make.

Summary
Right Bettors
Most Conservative:
1. Pass-line wager and full odds.
2. One come bet with full odds.
Conservative:
1. Pass-line wager with full odds.
2. Two come bets with full odds.
Aggressive:
1. Pass-line wager and full odds.
2. Two come bets and full odds.
3. Place bet on uncovered 6, 8, or both.

If a come bet is repeated and won during the course of a roll, then make another come bet immediately. In other words, the most conservative bettor will have a come bet always working, that is, being bet or in action. The conservative bettor will have two come bets always working, as will the most aggressive player.

Wrong Bettors
Most Conservative:
1. Don't pass bet, laying single odds.
Conservative:

1. Don't pass bet, laying single odds.
2. One don't come bet, laying single odds.

Aggressive:

1. Don't pass bet, laying single odds.
2. One don't come bet, laying single odds.
3. A second don't come bet, laying single odds.

Money Management

Money management is an integral part of any successful gambling method. You should never play with money you can't afford to lose, or that would cause you financial or emotional discomfort if you lost it.

Gambling should be fun and exciting. It won't be if you're too emotionally involved. If you are, do something else. Don't gamble. If you can handle the action, here's a system for knowing how much to bet:

Divide your bankroll by fifty, and make that your unit for betting purposes. In other words, if you bring $50 to the table, don't bet more than $1 as your basic unit. If you've got $100 to play with, you can be making $2 bets. Only if you have at least $250 should you be betting $5 at a time.

This is conservative betting, but it will allow you to stay at a craps table for a long time. It may allow you to catch a hot roll, if you're a right player, or a long, cold table, if you're a wrong bettor.

Try to double your money, and if you do that, quit. That's a good win in craps. If you can't do that, but you find that you're up $50 when you brought $100 to the table, and the game is choppy and going nowhere, leave.

Another good time to leave is at the end of a hot roll, if you're a right bettor. Hot rolls don't come often.

Conversely, if you're betting wrong, and the dice are ice cold, with only craps and point numbers coming up on the come-out, and 7s killing the point numbers time after time, leave when the dice start to turn so 7s and 11s begin to show on the come-out and a point is repeated.

What if you're losing? Set a limit to your losses. The best way is to play with a bankroll you can afford to lose in that session of play. If you lose your one-session bankroll, leave the table. Above all, don't reach in for more money after you've lost what you had in the rails.

The first loss is the cheapest. There'll be other games, other chances to win. There will always be time for more action at craps. Don't make the mistake of taking one truly terrible loss at one table. That's not the way smart gamblers handle losses.

Leave the table a winner if possible. A small win is better than any loss. You can't go wrong leaving a winner. Remember that. Now let's win!

Glossary of Craps Terms

Any Craps—A one-roll wager that the next throw of the dice will come up 2, 3 or 12, all craps numbers.

Any 7—A one-roll wager that the next throw of the dice will come up a 7.

Back Line—Another term for the **Don't Pass** line.

Barring the 12 (or 2)—Making either number a standoff for wrong bettors, thus enabling the casino to keep its edge on don't pass and don't come bets.

Betting Right—Betting that the dice will win, by wagering on the pass-line and come.

Betting Wrong—Wagering that the dice won't win (or pass), by betting on don't pass and don't come.

Big 6 and Big 8—An even-money wager that the 6 or 8, whichever is bet, will come up before a 7 is rolled.

Boxman—The casino employee who is in charge of an individual craps game. He is seated between the two dealers on base.

Buck—See **Disk.**

Buying the 4 and 10—Paying a 5% commission so the payoffs on these place numbers will be at 2-1.

Casino Advantage—See **Edge.**

Change Color—Changing casino chips into smaller or larger denominations.

Chips—The tokens, usually of clay composition, that are used by the players instead of cash; also known as **Casino Checks**.

Come Bet—A wager made after the come-out roll, according to the same rules as govern a pass-line bet.

Come-Out Roll—The roll that establishes a point for don't pass and pass-line bettors.

Craps—The term for the numbers 2, 3, and 12; also the name of the game.

Crap Out—Rolling a 2, 3 or 12 on the come-out.

Crew—The dealers who staff the craps table.

Dealer—A uniformed employee of the casino who is either on base or a stickman at the craps table.

Dice—The cubes marked from 1 to 6 which, when rolled by a shooter, determine all wins and losses in the game of casino craps.

Die—The singular of dice.

Disk—A white and black round object that, if unplaced, shows that there's a come-out roll about to happen, or, if placed, shows the point number; also known as **Buck, Marker Puck**.

Don't Come Bet—A wager against the dice made after the come-out roll, subject to the same rules as a Don't Pass bet.

Don't Pass Bet—A wager prior to the come-out roll that the dice won't win (or pass).

Double Odds Bet—A free-odds wager that is double the underlying bet.

Easy Way—The rolling of either 4, 6, 8 or 10 other than as a pair.

Edge—The advantage the house has on any wager; also known as **Casino Advantage** or **Vigorish**.

Even-Money—A payoff at odds of 1-1.

Field Bet—A one-roll wager that the next number thrown will be a 2, 3, 4, 9, 10, 11 or 12.

Floorman—A casino executive who supervises one or more craps tables.

Free-Odds Bet—A wager made in addition to an underlying bet that is paid off at correct odds.

Front Line—Another term for **Pass-Line**.

Hardway Bet—A wager that the 4, 6, 8 or 10 will be rolled as a pair before it's rolled easy or a 7 is thrown.

Horn Bet—A one-roll wager combining the numbers 2, 3, 11 and 12.

Hot Roll—A long series of dice throws where the pass-line and right bettors win.

Lay Wager—Betting against a point number's showing by paying a 5% commission.

Layout—The imprinted surface of a craps table, divided into separate areas, which shows all the wagers that can be made.

Marker Puck—See **Disk.**

Off—A term to signify that certain bets will not be in play on the next roll of the dice.

On Base—The term for the dealers other than the stickman.

One-Roll Bets—Wagers in effect for only the very next roll of the dice.

Pass—A winning decision for the right bettors.

Pass-Line Bet—A wager that the dice will win, or pass, made before the come-out roll.

Place Bets and Numbers—The wager that either one or more of the following numbers: 4, 5, 6, 8, 9, 10 will come up before a 7 is rolled.

Pit Boss—The casino executive in charge of all the craps tables comprising a craps pit.

Point, Point Number—The term for the number 4, 5, 6, 8, 9 or 10, when it's established on the come-out roll.

Press, Press A Bet—Increasing a winning

bet, usually by doubling it.

Proposition Bet, Center Bet—Those wagers which are made in the center of the layout.

Rails—The grooved area on top of the table where players keep their chips.

Right Bettor—A bettor who wagers that the dice will pass, or win.

Seven-Out—The rolling of a 7 after a point has been established, thus losing the pass-line wager.

Shooter—The player who is rolling the dice.

Single-Odds Bet—A free-odds wager equal to the underlying bet.

Stickman—The dealer who controls the dice and also calls the game.

Tip—A gratuity given to a dealer by a player; also called a **Toke**.

Vigorish—See **Edge.**

Working—A term used to describe bets in play or at risk on the next roll of the dice.

Wrong Bettor—A player who wagers that the dice will lose by making Don't Pass and Don't Come bets.

Winning Video Poker

Introduction

Video poker has become the most popular game played not only in gambling casinos and clubs, but also in bars, drugstores, supermarkets, gas stations and any other place else where these machines can be fitted into a vacant space. Their popularity is enormous, for the screen shows five cards from a deck, and the player will get payoffs depending on the final hand. In essence, it's draw poker played electronically.

The beauty of the game is that it can be beaten and can be played skillfully, unlike the slot machines, in which no skill is necessary. When you play video poker, you will be rewarded for correct play, and in this section we'll show you how to play correctly.

Having skill at this game pays off, not only in continual wins, but in jackpots as well. The jackpots can be lucrative, in the thousands of dollars for the quarter and dollar machines. Playing correctly and picking the right machines makes this game almost an even-up match between you and the casino.

In this chapter, I'm going to introduce you to the fascinating world of video poker, showing you all the games available to play, and which ones provide the best return on your money. If you follow my advice and play intelligently and sanely, you're going to end up a winner!

How to Play Video Poker

Introduction to Poker Hands

We'll briefly show the various hands you can be dealt, in descending order of strength, with the best hand listed first.

Royal Flush—A K Q J 10 of the same suit.

Straight Flush—Any five-card sequence in the same suit, such as J 10 9 8 7 or A 2 3 4 5.

Four-of-a-Kind—All four cards of the same rank, such as 7 7 7 7 and an odd card.

Full House—Three-of-a-Kind combined with a pair, such as 4 4 4 Q Q.

Flush—Any five cards of the same suit, but not in sequence.

Straight—Five cards in sequence, but not of the same suit, such as Q J 10 9 8 or A 2 3 4 5.

Three-of-a-Kind—Three cards of the same rank, with two odd cards, such as K K K 7 2.

Two Pair—Two separate pairs plus an odd card, such as 9 9 5 5 J.

One High Pair—Any pair, Js or better, with three odd cards, such as A A 9 6 4.

One Low Pair—Any pair below Js, with three odd cards, such as 5 5 K Q J.

No Pair—Five odd cards.

Some machines contain wild cards, such as a deuce (2) or a Joker. With these machines, Five-of-a-Kind hands have big payoffs, but rank below a Royal Flush.

Video Poker is basically draw poker, with all cards dealt out by the machine's computer. Initially, five cards are dealt to the player and are shown on the screen.

The player can now improve his hand by holding certain cards and discarding others. He could hold all five cards if he was dealt a Flush, for example, but discard an odd card if dealt a four-flush, such as A 9 8 5 of spades and a heart 3. In this instance, he would discard the 3 and hold the four spades, then draw for a possible improvement of his hand.

If dealt a spade, he would have a flush and be paid off. If dealt another A, he'd have a pair of As, a high pair, and be paid off for that hand. Another 9 8 or 5 wouldn't help because it's a low pair, below Js, and this hand would be a loser.

Let's follow another hand, and suppose that a player has received the following initial cards:

♠Q ♦7 ♣Q ♠3 ♥6

She has been dealt a pair of Qs, which she will hold, while discarding the rest of the cards. Under each card on the player's keyboard is a **hold button**, which, when pressed, will hold the card above it. If a player makes a mistake and presses this button incorrectly, he can press it again, and the **hold** disappears.

So now the two Qs are held, and the 7, 3 and 6 will be discarded and replaced by three new cards. Let's assume that the player's hand looks like this after the draw:

♠Q ♥Q ♣Q ♠K ♦4

She has improved her hand to Three-of-a-Kind, which means a bigger payout than the pair of Qs. The stronger the final poker hand, if it qualifies for a payout, the bigger the payout.

The machine deals out cards from a 52-card deck, and will never deal a card previously discarded on the same hand. Thus, if a player gets rid of the 6 of clubs, he can't get it back after the draw.

The final hand determines whether the player has won or lost. The board will flash **Winner** and sometimes show the kind of winning hand by flashing **Flush**, for instance. If the hand ended up as a losing hand, nothing will be flashed on the screen.

An important consideration, one that should always be kept in mind by the player, is that, although this is draw poker, it is not being played against other players. It is played against the machine, and all one has to do is get hands sufficient to be paid off.

A mistake many experienced draw poker players make is thinking they have to beat other players. They'll retain an A as a **kicker** with a small pair. That may be good play against other players, but it is a mistake in video poker. By holding the A they're taking away a spot for a card that can help the 9s possibly become three 9s or four 9s.

Or they'll discard a pair of 3s, thinking they're weak. They are weak but can improve, and it's much better to start with them than a blank screen, getting five new cards.

In regular draw poker, played against other players, it wouldn't pay to hold a small pair, but often, as we shall see later, it's the best play in Video Poker. Always keep in mind that you want to be paid off by the machine, not other players, and therefore, you'll have to alter your strategy to this effect.

Step by Step Play

When Video Poker machines were first introduced, it was necessary to start play by inserting coins into them. If you won a payout, you'd be rewarded with credits, which you could play off. When you ran out of credits, you'd have to put coins back in. Doing this slowed down the game considerably.

Today, to start the machine, you simply place a bill into a slot, either a $1, $5, $10, $20 or $100 bill, and once the machine scans and accepts the bill, credits flash on the machine. On a quarter machine, putting in $20 gives you 80 credits. A $100 bill gives you 400 credits.

On the machine there are buttons which are simple to operate and understand. You can bet the maximum 5 credits by pushing a button that states "maximum credits." Or you can play 1 credit or more by pushing a button that states "one credit." Each time you push this button, another credit shows up to 5.

We strongly suggest that you always play the maximum number of credits in order to possibly hit the best payout on Royal Flushes.

If you put a $20 bill into a quarter machine, you can play out the 80 credits, 5 at a time. Thus, you are able to play much faster. Once you press the maximum credit button, five cards will show on the screen, dealt in sequence. After examining the five cards of this hand, you can retain or discard whatever card or cards will give you the best chance at a payout.

At the same time, the screen will show you, the various payouts you can get, from a pair of Js or better, up to a Royal Flush.

To hold the cards you want to keep, you simply press the **hold button** under that particular card. On some modern machines you can touch the card on the screen to hold it.

Let's assume that your dealt cards are as follows:

♦3 ♥6 ♣7 ♠10 ♥10

The best chances to win are to hold the two 10s and discard the other cards. A pair of 10s won't give you a payout, but it can improve all the way to two pair or even Four-of-a-Kind. You now press the hold button under each 10 and "held" will appear under each 10 on the screen. Here's what the screen will now look like:

♦3 ♥6 ♣7 ♠10 ♥10

HELD HELD

Now that you're satisfied with your held cards, you press another button, called the **Deal/Draw** or **Deal** button. This will allow you to draw cards to the two held 10s. The 3, 6 and 7 will disappear from the screen and be replaced by the newly drawn cards. Your final hand may look like this:

♣J ♣A ♦J ♠10 ♥10

HELD HELD

You've improved to two pair, and the screen will show **Winner—Two Pair**. On most Js or better machines, you will receive a credit of 10 coins. Having started with 80 credits and having used 5 credits to play the hand, your credit total will now be 85.

Cashing Out

As you accumulate credits, another button on the machine will stay lit. This is the **Cashout** or **Payout** button. Whenever you want to cash out, press this button, your credits will be converted into coins and will fall into the metal area that takes such coins. It will completely use up your credits as coins.

At times, if you've been extremely lucky, you may deplete all the coins in the machine. When that happens, press the **Service** button and a casino employee will come and refill the machine with coins, so you can properly cash out.

On many modern machines, you can now also get paid by ticket, rather than by coins. You simply press the **Ticket** button, and your total credits will be shown on a ticket in dollars and cents.

For example, if you had 105 credits on a quarter machine, the ticket will read $26.25.

You take this ticket to a change booth for redemption in money, or you can play it at another machine that takes tickets in lieu of bills.

Some Representative Hands

What happens if you've been dealt a complete dud, five cards that are low in value and mismatched (**rags**) so that you don't want to hold any of them? You simply press the **Deal/ Draw** button and all five cards will disappear from the screen to be replaced by five different cards.

What if the five cards you've been dealt at the outset are such that you don't want to draw any cards to the hand? For example, let's assume that you've been dealt the following hand:

♦4 ♦A ♦3 ♦9 ♦8

You have five diamonds showing, a Flush, an immediate winner, without having to draw additional cards. What you do now is press the **Hold** button under each and every card shown, till there are five **HELDS** on the screen.

Then you press the **Deal/Draw** button, and you will see **Winner-Flush** show up on the screen. Some screens will also show the number of credits you've won.

If you have an immediate winner totaling five cards, such as a Flush before the draw, *you must hold all the cards to get the payoff.* If you don't press all the Hold buttons and simply press Deal/Draw, the winning cards will disappear from the screen and you'll get five fresh cards.

Now, for the ultimate win. What if you end up with a Royal Flush? You'll see **Winner–Royal Flush** on the screen. If it's a quarter machine that has a standard 4,000 coin jackpot, you'll collect that amount, but not from the machine. Lights will flash, and employees will come over quickly to verify the jackpot and pay you off in cash. Stay where you are and don't touch the machine. Guard it with your presence. If no employee shows up, ring for **Service.** A casino employee will come by.

On a progressive quarter machine, where the jackpot starts at $1,000 and goes higher with every play, you may see **Winner–Royal Flush** and the total win. Or just by looking at the progressive jackpot total on the top line, you'll see what you have won. If the win is over $1,200, you'll be asked to show ID or a social security number and you'll be handed cash along with a W-2G form to fill out and file with your income tax for that year.

When you get to a Video Poker machine, familiarize yourself with all the buttons before playing. If there's something you don't understand, ask a casino employee to explain it to you.

Now that you're ready to play Video Poker, let's move on to the most common of the machines, the one that originally made this game so popular, the Jacks or Better Video Poker machine.

Jacks or Better

Jacks or Better in Video Poker refers to a pair of Js, Qs, Ks or As. Since the Q, K or A is of a higher rank than the J, any pair consisting of these cards is known as Jacks or Better, or a High Pair.

If you get a pair of J, Q, K or A as your final hand, 5 credits (assuming you've bet 5) will be added to your total. For example, suppose you end up with a pair of Qs. You'll be declared a **Winner** and be given five credits.

Although you're not making any profit since you invested 5 credits in the play of the hand, these returned credits really add up and keep you in the game as you try for that jackpot!

Once you master Jacks or Better, you'll be able to play the other games of Video Poker more intelligently, and we'll discuss those games in future sections. But the Jacks or Better machines are the ones you're most likely to encounter, since they're the most popular of the Video Poker games.

At one time, when discussing Jacks or Better machines, we'd write about the **Full-Payout** or **Flat-Top** machine, and the **Progressive** machine. The Full-Payout or Flat-Top will pay you a fixed amount if you hit the Royal Flush—4,000 coins or credits on the quarter machines, provided that you bet all five credits, or the maximum wager.

With the Progressive machine, you'll be paid a jackpot consisting of the amount showing on the Progressive payout. This payment begins with 4,000 credits or coins or $1,000 on the quarter machines, and goes up from there. So, in most cases, if you hit the Royal Flush on the Progressive 25¢ machines, you can expect to cash in from $1,000 to about $3,000 and sometimes more.

Today, there are a number of other Jacks or Better machines with varying payouts, known by such names as **Bonus, Double Bonus, Double Double Bonus** and so forth. We'll cover these machines later on. For now, we'll concentrate on the Jacks or Better machines, both Flat Tops and Progressives, with a standard 8-5 payout.

The 8-5 Payouts

Most machines today, other than the bonus ones we'll discuss later, are 8-5 machines. This is what the pros call machines where the payout is 8 credits for each 1 credit played when a full house comes up, and 5 credit payouts for each 1 credit played when a flush is dealt. Let's look at a chart to see what these payouts look like, first with 1 credit played, and then with 5 credits wagered.

Jacks or Better–One Credit Bet	
Winning Hand	**Payout**
Royal Flush	Progressive or 800
Straight Flush	50
Four-of-a-Kind	25
Full House	8
Flush	5
Straight	4
Three-of-a-Kind	3
Two Pair	2
Jacks or Better	1

The next chart will show the maximum payouts with 5 credits wagered:

Jacks or Better–5 Credits Bet	
Winning Hand	**Payout**
Royal Flush	Progressive or 4,000
Straight Flush	250
Four-of-a-Kind	125
Full House	40
Flush	25
Straight	20
Three-of-a-Kind	15
Two Pair	10
Jacks or Better	5

Always play 5 coins with Progressive machines. These machines are tied to a bank of machines feeding the progressive jackpot every time a Royal Flush isn't made. The amount the jackpot increases varies, but it slowly but surely builds up from $1,000.

The jackpot total is shown above the bank of machines on a flashing screen that can be seen from quite a distance away in the casino. If you see a screen showing its quarter machines paying off over $2,000, head for them.

Progressive, as well as Flat-Tops, can be played for nickels, quarters or dollars. On a nickel machine, the jackpot starts at $200, while on the dollar machines, it begins at $4,000.

Winning Strategies for the 8-5 Jacks or Better Machines

The following is the correct basic strategy to be played on these machines.

Going For the Royal Flush

Your first goal is to get the Royal Flush, so each time there's a possibility of this occurring, you have to weigh the hands dealt against the chances of drawing to the Royal Flush. Here's your strategy.

1. Whenever you have <u>four cards to a Royal Flush</u>, such as ♣K ♣Q ♣J ♣10, discard the fifth card, even though it has given you a Straight or a Flush.

2. In the above example, if there was another

K, Q or J, giving us High Pair, you'd discard it, going for the Royal Flush.

3. When you have <u>three to a Royal Flush</u>, you discard a High Pair and draw to the remaining three cards to a Royal. This is in line with your goal of trying to get that Royal Flush whenever possible. For example, you're dealt ♦A ♥A ♥K ♥10 ♣3. You'd go for the three to a Royal Flush in this situation, breaking up the high pair and throwing away the ♦A and ♣3.

If however, you hold the following hands, hands that already have a payout on all cards dealt, you don't go for the Royal Flush.

a. Straight Flush.

b. Four-of-a-Kind.

c. Full House.

d. Three-of-a-Kind.

4. When holding <u>a small pair (10s or below) and three to a Royal Flush</u>, you discard the pair and go for the Royal Flush.

5. When you have only <u>two to a Royal Flush,</u> we hold all pairs over the possibility of going for the Royal Flush. For example, if you hold ♥A ♦A ♦Q and two **rags** (cards that can't help your hand) you retain the As rather than retaining the two high diamonds. If you hold a low pair and two to the Royal, you still hold onto the low pair, and discard the two cards to the Royal.

6. With <u>two to a Royal,</u> you hold onto four flushes and four straights, Three-of-a-Kind and two pair, rather than going for the Royal Flush.

7. If you have <u>two to a Royal</u> and another high card, but no pair, we discard the other high card. *This is an important move that should always be made.* For example, suppose you're dealt ♣Q ♦A ♦K and two rags. You discard the ♣Q and the two rags, going for the Royal with your A and K of diamonds. I have personally hit two Royals this way.

Always keep that Royal Flush in mind. It gives you the really big payout, and it's always lurking in the machine. You can't pass up the opportunity to go for it when the situation favors us.

Straight Flushes, Flushes & Straights

Your best payout, other than the Royal Flush, is the Straight Flush. Its' payout, however is merely 50 for 1 or 250 credits, against the Royal Flush's payoff of 4,000 credits or the big Progressive jackpot. Therefore, although we're likely to get a Straight Flush four times as often as a Royal Flush, the payout is only 1/16 of the Royal Flush, and even less if a Progressive jackpot hits.

Although you must be aware of the Straight Flush, it's not something you're constantly looking for, as in the case of the Royal.

When you are dealt a Flush, and it contains four to a Straight Flush, such as ♥10 ♥9 ♥8 ♥7 ♥2, your best play is to retain the Flush and not go for the Straight Flush. If dealt a Straight, and it contains four cards to a Straight Flush within it, discard the odd card and go for the Straight Flush. An example might be ♠7 ♠6 ♠5 ♠4 ♦3. We kiss off the ♦3.

A High Pair is always preferable to a four to a Flush or Straight. Retain the High Pair (Jacks or Better) and break up the possible Flush or Straight.

With a low pair, break up the low pair (10s or lower) in favor of the four to a Flush, but retain the low pair and break up the four to a Straight.

Four-of-a-Kinds, Full Houses & Three-of-a-Kinds

Four-of-a-Kind hands pay half of what Straight Flushes pay, but occur much more frequently, about once in every 420 hands, or about 22.7 times more frequently than the

Straight Flush. Since it pays half of what the Straight Flush pays, it's a much better value for you, coming up so often.

Sometimes, Four-of-a-Kind hands come out of the blue and surprise us. We start with a lowly pair of 3s and two more 3s come on the screen. Or you may stay with a Three-of-a-Kind hand and get the fourth of that rank. Sometimes, you'll really be surprised when you stay with one high card and get three more for a Four-of-a-Kind hand!

This is the main difference between regular Draw Poker and Video Poker. In the regular game, you wouldn't stay in with low pairs or just one high card, because it'll be a loser in the long run. In Video Poker you have nothing to lose, for you've already invested our money.

Three-of-a-Kind hands occur about once every thirteen times, or about 7.5% of the time. You may get them by being dealt them outright, or by drawing to a retained pair. Or perhaps if you're fortunate, you've stayed in with one high card and received two more of the same rank.

Always stay for the draw with a Three-of-a-Kind hand. It's much stronger for you than three to a Royal Flush, so, if you're dealt

♥K ♥Q ♥10 ♣10 ♦10, retain the three 10s and discard the K and Q of hearts.

A Full House is sometimes made from a Three-of-a-Kind hand, but the odds are roughly 11-1 against this happening. Of course, like all hands in Video Poker, a Full House can come out of the blue, where you've retained one low pair, such as ♦5 ♠5 and you see the screen fill up with ♣J ♦J ♠J.

A Full House occurs a little over 1% of the time.

Two Pair, High Pairs & Low Pairs

Two Pair hands occur about once every 7.6 hands and pays off with only 2 credits for each credit invested, or, in reality, at even-money. Thus, you get back 10 credits for the 5 credits played the 5 invested plus the 5 won. When you have Two Pair, go for the Full House by dumping the odd card, although the odds are about 10-1 against you getting it.

A High Pair allows you to get your original investment back. Although this doesn't sound like much, it's the reason for the game's popularity, since it enables players to constantly get payouts and thus retain their bankroll till the big payouts come through. You should be dealt a High Pair about once every 4.6 hands.

Retain the High Pair when it's part of a possible Straight or Flush, and discard the other cards in those situations. If the High Pair is part of a Straight Flush, such as ♦J ♦10 ♦9 ♦8 ♣J, then get rid of the ♣J and go for the Straight Flush. Do this even if the possible Straight Flush can be made by drawing to it as an inside Straight Flush, as in the following situation:

♥Q ♥J ♥10 ♥8 ♠Q

In the above example, the ♠Q would be discarded. There's a chance for a Straight Flush, a Flush, a Straight and another High Pair when this is done, giving you more powerful hands to go for, with bigger payouts.

With small pairs, you have hands that can give you many payouts when they are improved. Normally in regular draw poker, only a very weak player would retain a pair of 4s, but in Video Poker, those 4s can turn into Three-of-a-Kind hands or better if we get a lucky draw.

Retain the small pairs when you have three rags in the same hand, or in the following hand:

♥A ♠K ♥J ♠5 ♦5

Hold onto the 5s and discard the three high cards. Retain the small pair in a four Straight hand, but get rid of it in a Four Flush hand. If they are part of a three to a Straight Flush, such as ♦8 ♦7 ♦6 ♠6 ♥K, retain the small pair of 6s.

Other Hands

Most of the time, the hands dealt to you before the draw won't be winners by themselves. You'll have to improve them to get a payout. At times, you'll find yourself with a powerful drawing hand that comes up empty. For example:

♠A ♠Q ♠K ♠J ♦3

Having four to a Royal Flush, discard the ♦3 and hit the Draw button, hoping for the **BIG ONE!** Instead you're dealt the 9 of hearts and end up without a payout of any kind. Other good hands will end up as blanks for you. This is to be expected. Don't get discouraged. There will be other times, like the one there was for this author, when the following hand was dealt to him:

♦4 ♥7 ♦9 ♠2 ♣J

Faced with this pile of garbage I retained the ♣J, the only viable play. Imagine my surprise when I drew four cards and saw the following on the screen:

♣K ♣Q ♣10 ♣A ♣J
HELD

And on the screen were these words:
WINNER! JACKPOT! ROYAL FLUSH!

Many times you'll get a hand like this:

♦4 ♥A ♣J ♠6 ♥3

Hold the A and the J, for we're trying to pair one of these to get at least 5 credits. Many players make the mistake of retaining only the A and discarding the J. That's a bad play. Hold onto both. Remember, in Video Poker, any High Card that is paired will pay off. In this regard, an A is no stronger than a J.

We already have discussed holding four to a Straight Flush (whether open-ended or gut shot) four to a Flush and four to a Straight. If you're dealt three to a Straight Flush, discard the rags and go for it. If the hand contains a High Card as part of the Straight Flush, it is that much stronger, such as ♦J ♦10 ♦9, since the J may be paired even if you miss any other hand after the draw.

With low pairs, retain them in the hope of getting a monster hand, such as Four-of-a-Kind, or any payout. Suppose you see ♣5 ♦5 ♥A ♣J ♦10. Here, you hold the pair of 5s. Lots of times you won't improve, but there will be times when you get a good payout for this play.

Now let's deal with those hands that are so bad there's no reason to hold any of the cards. When you get five blanks or rags, hold nothing and go for five new cards on the draw. Such a hand might be:

♥2 ♦6 ♣10 ♦8 ♥4

There's nothing worth holding. To get five new cards, simply press the Deal/Draw button and five new cards will appear on the screen. Don't be afraid to get rid of all five cards. As the poker pros say, "Muck them." There's always a chance of getting a payoff of some kind. The biggest hand I ever got after mucking the five cards was four 6s. By some miracle, you might even get a Royal Flush doing this!

Some Winning Hints

One of the important differences between regular Draw Poker and Video Poker is this—when you play Draw Poker you're able to sort your cards in the proper order. If you've been dealt a pair, you put them side by side. If you have been dealt four to a Straight, you place those cards in their proper sequence.

However, when playing Video Poker, the cards come up on the screen just as the computer deals them and the player must carefully see just what has been dealt. So you have to be super careful about not overlooking a strong hand. Most machines will immediately show what you have, by changing color on one of the lines.

For example, if the payout lines are in yellow, the line showing the winning hand will appear in white. If you've been dealt Two Pair, for example, that line will change color. But many players play the game at a rapid pace and sometimes overlook this indication.

I watched a player muck these cards before the draw:

$$\spadesuit 5 \quad \heartsuit 6 \quad \clubsuit 3 \quad \spadesuit 2 \quad \spadesuit 4$$

He simply overlooked the Straight. Another player, dealt a wheel (a Straight from A to 5) retained only the A and overlooked his made Straight.

Therefore, my best advice is to slow down a bit, examine the cards that have been dealt to you at the outset, and see just what you have on the screen.

Take your time in determining the correct play. If you do make a mistake and hold the wrong card, you can rectify that mistake by pressing the Hold button again, negating the previous hold. As long as you don't press the Deal/Draw button, you still have a chance to make any changes necessary.

Even experienced veterans of the game

make mistakes. They may be weary or tired or upset, and they can, in this state, overlook obvious plays. If you reach a point where the game has become tedious, leave the machine and cash in. Take a break and go back another time when you're refreshed and ready to play.

A final note: when playing progressive machines, avoid those with payouts that indicate the jackpot has recently been hit. The progressives start at $1,000. If you're in a casino where the payouts are $1,092 and $1,100, don't play these machines. You want to play those that haven't been hit for awhile.

Practicing at Home

In earlier editions of this book, I suggested practicing at home by dealing out cards by hand. But now, if you have a computer, the best way to practice is to buy software that contains Video Poker and other casino games, and play on your computer. There is generally an "expert advice" section on these games. Cardoza Publishing makes a fine software program which I highly recommend.

At home, you should make sure that you have the basic strategy of the game down pat. If you make a mistake, it won't cost you money. You'll learn fast this way, and using this book as a guide, you'll easily become an expert player. After you're comfortable with the game and know what you're doing, you can go to a casino and play for real money.

Testing Your Knowledge of Jacks or Better

The following is a small quiz to refine and test your knowledge of the game played in the casino. We'll assume that we're at a machine that has an 8-5 payout on the Full House and Flush, respectively. Decide how to play each of the following hands:

1. ♣5 ♦5 ♠A ♠9 ♦10

Hold the pair of 5s and discard the other cards. We never save a "kicker" such as the A in Video Poker.

2. ♦9 ♦K ♣K ♦8 ♦2

Hold the Ks and discard the other diamonds. Always hold the High Pair as opposed to drawing for a possible Flush.

3. ♣K ♣Q ♣A ♣10 ♠J

With four to the Royal Flush, discard the spade J. Whenever you have four to a Royal, you're going for the jackpot.

4. ♠Q ♦3 ♠J ♥K ♥2

This kind of hand comes up frequently. Retain the Q and J of spades, and kiss off the other cards. You can possibly make a Royal

Flush here, and don't want the K of hearts in the way.

5. ♠9 ♠5 ♠2 ♣8 ♣3

There is nothing worthwhile in this pile of junk. Even though you have three to a Flush in spades, there's no reason to overcome the great odds of drawing to it. You're better off going for five fresh cards after the draw.

6. ♠10 ♣8 ♦3 ♠J ♠4

At first glance, it would seem correct to hold the spade J and discard the other cards. Or you could go for a long shot and hold all three spades. Both of these decisions are incorrect. Hold the J and 10 of spades, giving us two to a Royal.

7. ♠2 ♠A ♣K ♦J ♣2

We hold the deuces and discard the three High Cards. A small pair is powerful in Video Poker, because it can improve dramatically, even to a Four-of-a-Kind hand. In this instance, don't chase a possible pairing of a High Card, and we don't hold kickers.

8. ♥Q ♥J ♠10 ♠4 ♠3

You have both a three to a Flush and a Straight. However, you also have a Q and J, which, if either is paired, will get us five credits. You therefore hold the Q and J and discard the other cards.

9. ♠J ♠K ♠9 ♠Q ♥9

You have three to a Royal Flush plus a small pair of 9s. Get rid of a small pair in this situation and go for the Royal.

10. ♥K ♥Q ♥J ♥A ♥5

Here you have four to a Royal and a formed Flush. In this situation, get rid of the heart 5 and go for the Royal. Why? Just look at the odds. Suppose the Progressive payout at this point is $1,600. When you put in $1.25, your payout is 1,280 for 1. Now, if you get rid of the 5 of hearts, your chances of getting the Royal are only 46-1 to get a payment of 1,280 for 1. You'll take that any day of the week.

Well, that's our quiz. Just a representative group of questions, but of course, there is much more to the game. My suggestion: if you want to learn Video Poker so you can play on a professional level and actually have an edge over the casino, buy the excellent advanced strategy listed in the back of this book.

Bonus, Double Bonus & Double Double Bonus

In recent years, new forms of Video Poker have sprung up, and some of the more common games are known as Bonus games, either single, double or double double.

WINNING VIDEO POKER

You can find these games in practically all casinos, and they may be found as individual Video Poker games, or as part of a Multi-Poker format, where the casino or store allows you to touch the screen and pick the game of your choice.

Also, Game King™ machines, manufactured by IGT, give you a choice of the same games. If you want to change games, all you have to do is press a button which says "more games" or "other games" and once more you'll see the screen in order to make a new selection.

Some of these games have progressive jackpots, while most are of the flat-top variety with a fixed payout of 4,000 credits or coins if the jackpot is hit with the player wagering 5 credits or coins and getting a Royal Flush.

Many of the Multi-Poker machines can be paid off by coins or by a ticket, which is brought to the change cashier. Of course, jackpots are paid off by a casino employee at the machine, with cash.

Here is a typical payout schedule for a Bonus Poker machine.

Bonus Poker Payouts–5 Credits Bet	
Winning Hand	**Payout**
Royal Flush	4,000 or Progressive
Straight Flush	250
Four As	400
Four 2s, 3s or 4s	200
Four 5s through Kings	125
Full House	35
Flush	25
Three-of-a-Kind	15
Two Pair	10
Jacks or Better	5

We can ascertain the differences between these payouts and those of ordinary 8-5 Jacks or Better machines. First of all, this is a 7-5 machine, with only 35 credits for a Full House.

The bonus feature is in the payouts for Four As and Four 2s, 3s and 4s. A normal Jacks or Better machine pays all Four-of-a-Kind hands with 125 credits. Here, with four As, the payout is 400 credits or 3.2 times the ordinary payout. And the four 2s, 3s or 4s are paid off with 200 credits, or 1.6 times the ordinary payout.

With these payouts in mind, you must alter our basic strategy when playing the bonus machine. First of all, if you have an A and another high card of a different suit dealt to you, retain just the A. You would also retain a pair of 2s through 4s, rather than discarding them and going for a Flush.

Play the Progressive Bonus machines, if you can find them. With the popularity of Video Poker, the manufacturers and casinos have gone more and more to Flat-Tops, with a standard 4,000 credit or coin payout. In the early days of Video Poker, there were plenty of progressive machines with some great payouts. Now they're harder to find.

At first glance, the Double Bonus seems a much better deal for the player than the Bonus Poker machine. Payouts for Four-of-a-Kind hands are double. And this is a 9-6 machine (payouts on the Full House and Flush) rather than a 7-5 machine.

Double Bonus Payouts–5 Credits Bet	
Winning Hand	**Payout**
Royal Flush	4,000 or Progressive
Straight Flush	250
Four As	800
Four 2, 3s or 4s	400
Four 5s through Kings	250
Full House	45
Flush	30
Straight	20
Three-of-a-Kind	15
Two Pair	5
Jacks or Better	5

The rub is the payout for the Two Pair, which is even-money, rather than 2 for 1. This makes a difference, for Two Pair hands normally occur every 7.6 hands. Getting the smaller payout makes a tremendous difference, for the small payouts are what keep us in the game, and keep our bankroll fresh.

When playing Double Bonus, focus on the Four-of-a-Kind hands, especially the As, with $200 payoff on a quarter machine.

With an A and another big card of a different suit, retain only the A. With the 2s, 3s and 4s, these small pairs can give us $100 if they develop into Four-of-a-Kind hands, and so, when you have a four Flush, and a pair of 2s, 3s or 4s, save the small pair, and don't go for the Flush. Any pair is favored over the possible Flush, and certainly over the possible Straight.

If dealt Two Pair at the outset, retain only the High Pair (Jacks or Better) and discard the smaller ones in a hand such as Q Q 6 6. It's approximately 10-1 against getting the Full House, and generally you'll be getting only your even-money payout after the draw.

With the High Pair, you can improve to a big Four-of-a-Kind payout, while guaranteeing even-money payout for Jacks or Better.

This machine following is an 8-5 machine, with only even-money payouts for Two Pair hands. The dazzling payout of 2,000 credits or coins for Four As with a 2, 3 or 4 is quite seductive here, as is the 800 credit payout for Four As, or for Four 2s, 3s, 4s with an A, 2, 3 or 4. Suppose you are extremely lucky and are dealt the following hand at the outset:

♣A ♠A ♦A ♥A ♦8

With an ordinary Jacks or Better machine, you'd press **HELD** under all the cards, and get your payout. But not here. You must get rid of the ♦8 and hold the As. If you're fortunate enough to get a 2, 3 or 4 of any suit, you'd receive a payout of 2,000 credits ($500) instead of 800 credits ($200). You must be alert to this when playing the Double Double Bonus machines.

Double Double Bonus–5 Credits Bet	
Winning Hand	**Payout**
Royal Flush	4,000 or Progressive
Straight Flush	250
Four As with a 2, 3 or 4	2,000
Four As	800
Four 2s, 3s or 4s with A, 2, 3, 4	800
Four 2s, 3s or 4s	400
Four 5s through Kings	250
Full House	40
Flush	25
Straight	20
Three-of-a-Kind	15
Two Pair	5
Jacks or Better	5

The same principle holds true when dealt four 2s, 3s or 4s at the outset. You must kiss off the odd card unless it's an A, 2, 3 or 4, and try to double your credits from 400 to 800.

With a Double Double Bonus machine, you'll find your money draining away unless you can hit one of the big hands. The even-money for Two Pair and the 8-5 payout for the Full House and Flush penalize the player otherwise.

Triple Play and Five Play Machines

These machines are somewhat popular because they allow a player to gamble at either three or five Video Poker games at the same time. With Triple Play, one open hand is shown on the screen, and the player holds those cards that will give him the biggest possible payout. This is done on the bottom or "A" line.

For example, he might hold two Ks, and thus each of the three hands will show the two Ks. Then he draws three cards to each of the hands to improve. With big hands there are triple payouts, but of course, if his or her luck goes badly, the losses mount rapidly, because 15 coins or credits are being bet at one time for the maximum payouts.

With Five Play, five hands are played this way, and that means 25 coins or credits bet at one time. These machines are built to be bet with either nickels, dimes, quarters or half-dollars. No coins need be used, for credits will be awarded after a bill is slipped into the machine.

The Triple Play and Five Play payouts are pretty much the same, with maximum 4,000 credit payouts. The following chart will show them for a Bonus machine.

Triple Play & Five Play Bonus Payouts–5 Credits Bet	
Winning Hand	**Payout**
Royal Flush	4,000
Straight Flush	250
Four As	400
Four 2s 3s or 4s	200
Four 5s through Kings	125
Full House	40
Flush	25
Straight	20
Three-of-a-Kind	15
Two Pair	10
Jacks or Better	5

These 8-5 machines without a progressive jackpot are not recommended for play except for those who want to do some gambling, in the hope of getting some big payouts paid three or five times at once.

Deuces Wild

Like the other versions of Video Poker, Deuces Wild is played with an ordinary 52-card deck. However, each of the four deuces (2s) is a **wild card**, which means it can be used as any card in the deck, not only in rank (such as the K or Q, for example) but as any suit. Since there are four deuces in the deck, hands containing at least one deuce have been calculated to occur about 35% of the time.

Note that the weakest possible hand with a payout is Three-of-a-Kind. And a Five-of-a-Kind hand pays only 15 for 1! That's a pretty shabby payoff. With the deuces running wild in the deck, all kinds of crazy hands can be made and a lot of the payouts are penalized, especially for the weaker hands.

Playing Deuces Wild can be a roller coaster ride with wild streaks coming and going, both favorable and unfavorable. When the deuces show up on the screen, all kinds of payouts are possible. When they're absent, it's a desert out there, because of the low payouts on relatively strong hands, such as even-money on a Three-of-a-Kind hand.

Even when dealt one deuce, your chances of making a hand that pays out are only 54%. When you're dealt three deuces, you're assured of at least a Four-of-a-Kind hand, but even this pays only 20 credits.

The following chart shows the payout schedule for Deuces Wild Video Poker.

Deuces Wild Payout–Five Credits Bet	
Winning Hand	**Payout**
Royal Flush (no 2s)	4,000 or Progressive
Four Deuces	1,000
Royal Flush with Deuce	100
Five-of-a-Kind	60
Straight Flush	45
Four-of-a-Kind	20
Full House	20
Flush	15
Straight	10
Three-of-a-Kind	5

Deuces Wild Strategy

1. If we have three deuces and two to a Royal Flush, that's a Royal Flush and should be held intact.

2. With two deuces and three to a Royal, this hand should be held intact as a Royal Flush.

3. Two deuces and a Three-of-a-Kind hand is a Five-of-a-Kind hand and should be held intact.

4. If we have two deuces and three cards to a Straight Flush, this hand should be held intact. If it's merely a flush, save only the two deuces.

5. With two deuces and three odd cards, none

of which can give you a Royal Flush, draw three cards to the deuces.

6. With a single deuce and three to a Royal Flush, plus an odd card, we discard the odd card and draw one card.

7. Without a deuce, if the hand gives us a payout with all five cards intact, we hold the hand and don't draw.

8. Without a deuce, we hold the following hands: four to a Straight Flush, four to a Flush and four to a Straight, discarding the odd card.

9. Without a deuce, we hold three-card Straight Flushes and draw.

10. With hands such as ♦A ♥K ♠Q ♦4 ♥8, we discard all the cards.

Pairing any of the big cards or even making two pair gives us nothing. You'll find you'll often, up to 25% of the time, be discarding all the cards dealt to you.

Play the game correctly, and you'll be rewarded with all kinds of big hands, and if you encounter a good winning streak, this game can earn you some good money even without hitting the Royal Flush.

Jokers Wild

This game is played often on a nickel or quarter machine and some IGT machines call it "Joker Poker." The single Joker in the deck is a wild card and can be used for any ranked card or suit to make the best possible poker hand. The following chart shows a typical payout schedule for the quarter game.

Jokers Wild Payout–Five Credits Bet	
Winning Hand	**Payout**
Royal Flush	4,000 or Progressive
Five-of-a-Kind	1,000 or Progressive
Royal Flush with Joker	500
Straight Flush	250
Four-of-a-Kind	75
Full House	35
Flush	25
Straight	15
Three-of-a-Kind	10
Two Pair	5
Kings or Better	5

With the addition of the Joker, we now have a deck containing 53 cards, with approximately 10% more different kinds of hands dealt out than in the 52-card standard Video Poker games.

The lack of payout below a pair of Ks makes this machine a tough one to beat. When the Joker doesn't appear at the outset, before the draw, there are going to be many hands that will not get any payout whatsoever.

Joker Wild: Kings or Better Strategy

The Joker will appear in the hand less than 10% of the time, or about 9.4%. Many times, without the Joker, we'll simply have to discard all five cards dealt at the outset. Since only As and Ks are good as High Pairs, we don't retain a Q or J. They're as useless as an odd 9 or 4.

• We will break up a formed Straight to go for a Straight Flush, if no Joker has been dealt at the outset. Among hands to be discarded whole before the draw are the following:

• Two cards to a Flush.

• Three cards to a Flush, unless it gives us a chance at a Royal Flush or a Straight Flush, such as A J 10 suited or 9 7 6 suited.

• With the Joker present, there is a good chance to get a Straight Flush, and we get rid of a completed Flush in a hand such as this, to go for the Straight Flush.

Jkr ♥6 ♥7 ♥5 ♥Q

With the above hand, we dump the Q of hearts and draw one card. When we have three to a Straight Flush with the Joker, as above, we retain these four cards and get rid of a high card, going for the Straight Flush rather than being satisfied with a Flush or a High Pair payout.

• When dealt the Joker at the outset, we'll retain only the Joker even if the hand has two suited cards. We discard the possible Flush. The same is true for a possible Royal Flush.

• Hands to hold are Three-of-a-Kind, Straights and Flushes, formed before the draw.

Joker Wild is a complicated game, and is best studied at home without money, by using software on your computer or dealing out hands with a joker in the deck. Unless you feel comfortable with the game, I'd stick to simpler Video Poker versions.

Money Management

The Bankroll

You should feel comfortable financially and emotionally playing Video Poker machines because you may find yourself losing at the outset. Unless you get some big hands, the money in your possession may just dribble away.

I would start with $20 on the nickel machines, $100 on the quarter machines and $300 on the dollar machines. If any of these bankrolls will hurt you financially, don't gamble on Video Poker.

Practically all machines now take bills, and some tickets that can be used in lieu of cash. Most machines still pay out in coins, so make certain that you have a bucket nearby to use when you cash out. Don't leave the machine either with credits on it or coins in the well. Ring the bell for service and have a casino employee bring you one of the casino's paper buckets.

When to Quit

A gambling principle well worth memorizing is this: *the first loss is the cheapest.*

If you lose your initial bankroll, don't start looking for an ATM machine. Stop playing. The machine has been cruel to you, and enough is enough. There are other machines that will be kind; that will give you constant payouts and some big ones at that. There's nothing sweeter, other than hitting the Royal Flush, to keep getting Full Houses and Four-of-a-Kind hands, with the credits mounting up into the high 100s.

No matter how many credits you have, make sure to cash out. You will either get coins or a printed ticket which will say "Cash-Out" and show the name of the casino, the date, the amount of the ticket in terms of cash, and a notice that it expires in 60 days.

What you don't want to do is have a big win, a ton of credits, and then watch the machine turn sour and those credits evaporate. Make a decision to get away as a winner. Suppose you're ahead 380 credits on a quarter machine. 300 credits add up to $75. If you go down that far, cash out. I've seen players lose their 380 credits, take more money from their wallets and end up with a frightening loss. *Leave a winner*, if possible.

Sometimes a machine will fool you. I was in a downtown Las Vegas casino and had the choice of two quarter machines, the end one or the one next to it. I was waiting for a friend to take to lunch, and figured I'd take a shot with $20. It was a progressive paying about $1,600. As I stood there, a middle-aged man took the end machine, so I sat down at the other one and slid in the $20 bill.

My neighbor chuckled as he was dealt a Full House. I got zilch. Then he got another Full House. I was rewarded with nothing. He followed this with a Flush, then Three-of-a-Kind and another Full House. I looked at my watch. I had about five minutes to go before my friend would show up. And was down to 10 credits. Well, there went the $20, I thought, and then the following hand was dealt:

♦A   ♠Q   ♦10   ♥5   ♥4

I saved the A and 10 of diamonds. Instinctively I always go for the possible Royal. As my neighbor hit a Straight, I tapped the Deal/Draw button and looked at the screen: **A Royal Flush! WINNER!**

There was this beautiful hand showing:

♦A ♦K ♦10 ♦J ♦Q
HELD   HELD

A casino employee paid me off just as my friend arrived for lunch. I wished my neighbor good luck and we were on our way to a buffet lunch, which the casino comped without my asking.

Glossary of Video Poker Terms

Bonus Poker—A form of Jacks or Better where bonuses are paid for certain dealt hands.

Cash Out Button—A button that releases all the credits and drops all previously won coins into the well. On some modern machines, a ticket showing the cash value of the credits is issued.

Cash Out Ticket—A ticket issued by the machine showing the cash value of the credits. This machine can be used on other machines in lieu of bills.

Cashier Cage—A place on the casino floor where players can receive cash for their coins or cash-out tickets.

Changeperson—A casino employee who makes change and roams through the casino floor for this purpose. With the advent of machines that accept bills and tickets, changepersons are becoming obsolete.

Credit/Max Credit Button—The Credit button, when pressed, plays one credit at a time. The Max Credit button plays five credits or whatever the maximum bet is.

Deal/Draw Button—This button, when pressed, causes the machine to issue a new hand if fewer than the maximum credits have been bet. It is also used, when the maximum credits are bet, to issue cards after the draw.

Deuces Wild—A form of Video Poker where each of the four 2s are wild cards.

Double Bonus/Double Double Bonus Poker—Forms of Video Poker where bonuses are paid for certain dealt hands such as Four As.

Five-of-a-Kind—This hand is possible when playing a wild card game, such as Deuces Wild or Jokers Wild.

Five Play Machine—A machine that plays five hands of Video Poker at the same time.

Flattop Machines—These machines have a fixed maximum payout for a Royal Flush, usually 4,000 credits or coins.

Four Flush—A hand consisting of four cards

of the same suit, together with an odd card. Example: ♦4 ♦9 ♦10 ♦K ♥5

Four-of-a-Kind—A hand consisting of four cards of the same rank such as 9 9 9 9.

Four Straight—A hand consisting of four cards, not of the same suit, but in sequence, such as ♦3 ♥4 ♣5 ♠6 together with an odd card. This is also known as an open-ended straight.

Full House—A hand that consists of a pair and Three-of-a-Kind, such as 8 8 J J J.

Gutshot Straight—A hand consisting of four cards to a possible straight, needing an interior card to form the straight, such as ♣8 ♦9 ♠J ♦Q.

High Card—J, Q, K or A, which, if paired in Jacks or Better and some other Video Poker games, will pay back the original bet to the player.

Hold Button—A button that, if pressed, will hold a particular card to the original hand dealt, so that it won't be replaced by the draw.

Jokers Wild—A form of Video Poker that has a Joker in addition to the regular 52-card deck. The Joker is a wild card in this game.

Kicker—A high, odd card which is held before the draw. An example might be an A held with a pair of 3s. Not recommended in Video Poker.

WINNING VIDEO POKER

Low Pair—A pair, usually 10s or lower ranked cards, which doesn't qualify for a payout in Jacks or Better poker.

Multi-Play Machine—A machine which offers a number of Video Poker games. The player chooses his game by touching the game shown on the screen.

Original Hand—The first five cards dealt to a player before he draws cards to improve the hand.

Progressive Machines—Video Poker machines whose jackpot is not fixed, but increases each time a Royal Flush isn't hit.

Rags/Blanks—Cards that are useless in forming a particular poker hand.

Royal Flush—The best hand in video poker; consists of the A, K, Q, J and 10 of the same suit.

Straight—Five cards in consecutive sequence but not of the same suit, such as 7, 8, 9, 10 and J. Also A, 2, 3, 4 and 5 as well as 10, J, Q, K and A.

Straight Flush—Five cards in sequence and of the same suit but without an A, such as ♦7 ♦8 ♦9 ♦10 ♦J.

Three-of-a-Kind—A hand consisting of three cards of the same rank, such as 4 4 4, together with two odd cards.

Triple Play—A form of Video Poker in which

three hands are bet and played at the same time.

Two Pair—A hand consisting of two separate pairs, such as K K 5 5, together with an odd card.

Well—The metal area in the bottom of the machine to which paid out coins fall.

Winning Poker

Introduction

Welcome to one of the greatest games ever invented by man—poker!

Poker is one of the most fascinating of the gambling games because it combines three elements: skill, luck and psychology. It is this combination which draws millions of players to the card tables around America to try their luck at poker.

Not only will you learn the most popular poker games, but with each game we also supply a great deal of strategy, which should give you an immediate edge over less skillful players. You'll learn which hands to go in with, how to bet, when to play aggressively and when to be cautious.

The games presented are those in which a great deal of money can be made by skillful players. You'll be learning the games by reading this chapter, but more importantly, you'll be learning how to be a winner.

The Fundamentals of Poker

Certain things are common to all poker games, and we'll now discuss them, so that when we cover the individual games, you'll be familiar with these aspects of the game.

The Deck of Cards

All the poker games we're going to discuss in this chapter will be played with a 52-card deck, containing four suits of 13 cards apiece. The suits are both black and red. The black suits are spades and clubs; the red ones are hearts and diamonds. In poker, the suits have no intrinsic value in determining winning hands. A flush in spades is not stronger than one in hearts, and a straight in clubs isn't weaker than one in diamonds.

The Four Suits

♠ ♥ ♦ ♣

What is important is the rank of the cards. As we mentioned, there are thirteen cards in each suit. The highest-ranking card is the A, followed in rank by the King as K, the Queen as Q and the Jack as J. All other cards, from 10-2, will be shown by the numeral, so that an eight will simply be shown as an 8. The numbered cards rank in value as follows, in descending order: 10, 9, 8, 7, 6, 5, 4, 3, and finally the 2, known as the **deuce**, which is the lowest ranking card of all.

Rank of the Hands—High Poker

Poker can be played as either high or low poker. Most of the games are played as high, such as **Seven-Card Stud**, **Hold 'em**, and so forth. There is also a game called **Lowball**, which is usually played as a draw game, or closed game, in which the cards are reversed in value, with the best card being the A and the weakest card the K. This type of game is called low poker and will be discussed under the rank of the hands section. For now, we'll concentrate on high poker and show the relative ranks of the hands, in descending order, from best to worst.

Royal Flush

This is the top hand in high poker, and a player may see it only once or twice in his lifetime. It consists of the A, K, Q, J and 10 *all of one suit*. For example, if these cards were all diamonds, spades, clubs or hearts, it would be a royal flush. If the same hand were of different suits, it would have a weaker ranking, and simply be an A–high straight.

Royal Flush

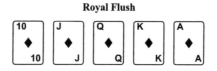

Straight Flush

This hand consists of five cards of consecutive rank, all of one suit, but with the top-ranking card lower than an A. For example, the K Q J 10 9 of diamonds would be a straight flush. Likewise the 5 4 3 2 A of clubs. For purposes of straights, as in a straight flush, the A is either the highest or lowest card. Thus, a hand of 2 A K Q J and a hand of 4 3 2 A K would not be straights nor straight flushes.

Straight Flush

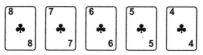

When two players have a straight flush, the one with the highest-ranking card leading the hand would win the pot. A hand of 8 7 6 5 4 of clubs would beat out a hand of 7 6 5 4 3 of spades because the 8 is higher ranked than the 7. If both straight flushes are identical, the pot is split.

Four-of-a-Kind

This hand contains four cards of the same

rank, such as J J J J, along with an odd card.

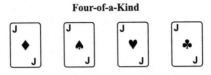

Four-of-a-Kind

There cannot be ties with four-of-a-kind hands, and when two players have these hands, the highest ranked card wins the pot. Four 9s will beat out four 8s.

Full House

This hand consists of Three-of-a-Kind, combined with a pair, 999 AA; 666 KK and QQQ 22 are all full houses.

Full House

If two or more players have full houses, then the player holding the highest ranked Three-of-a-Kind wins the pot. JJJ 99 will beat out 777 AA.

Flush

A hand of five cards of the same suit is called a flush. K Q 6 4 3 of diamonds would be a flush, and it would be called a K high flush since its highest ranked card is a K. The best flush is an **A high** flush.

Flush

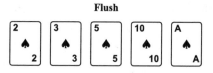

When two players have flushes, the highest ranked card in the flush determines the winner. If both have, for example, a Q high flush, then the next ranked card determines the winner, and so forth, till a winner is found. 10 9 8 5 4 as a flush beats out a flush of 10 9 8 5 3. If all five cards are identical, the pot is split.

Straight

Five cards in sequence, but not of the same suit, constitute a straight. For example, Q J 10 9 8 of mixed suits is a straight. An A-high straight of A K Q J 10 is the highest possible. The lowest possible straight is 5 4 3 2 A, with the A here as the lowest card.

Straight

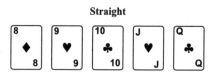

The highest ranking straight wins when two players have straights. If both straights are identical, the pot is split.

Three-of-a-Kind

This hand contains three cards of identical rank plus two odd cards. 333 K4 and QQQ 92 are Three-of-a-Kind hands.

Three-of-a-Kind

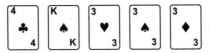

When two players hold Three-of-a-Kind hands, the highest ranking wins. Three Qs will beat out three Js.

Two Pair

This hand contains two separate pairs of identically ranked cards plus an odd card. AA 55 2 and QQ 88 K are two-pair hands.

Two Pair

If two players hold this kind of hand, then the highest ranking of pairs would win. If one player holds **As up**, and the other **Qs up**, as in the example of two pair hands above, the As up hand would win.

Should players hold identical high pairs, the other pair is taken into consideration to determine a winner. Should both pairs be identical, such as two players holding 77 22, then the odd card is examined and the highest ranking odd card wins, (77 22 5 beats out 77 22 4). If all five cards are identical, the pot is split.

One Pair

A pair and three odd cards make up this hand. 55 AQJ and 77 843 are both one-pair hands. If two players hold a pair, then the highest ranking pair wins. If the pairs are identical, then the highest ranking odd card determines who wins the pot. 99 QJ8 will beat out 99 QJ7.

One Pair

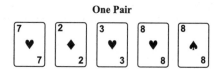

If all five cards are identical, the pot is split.

No Pair

When a player holds five odd cards, not of the same suit, he has the weakest of all poker hands. When two or more players hold this hand, the highest ranked card wins the pot. If this is identical, then the next card is examined and so forth. J 9 8 5 3 beats out J 9 8 5 2.

If all five cards are identical, the pot is split.

Jack-High Hand

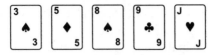

To recapitulate: if there are several players at the **showdown**, which is the point where hands are shown to determine who wins the pot, then the highest ranking hand wins automatically. If one player has a Straight and the other two have Three-of-a-Kind, the straight would win.

Object of the Game

To state it as simply as possible, the object of poker is to win the money in the pot. The **pot** is the accumulation of antes and bets made by the players. There are two basic ways to win the pot. The first and most common way is to have the best hand at the showdown. The showdown is the moment after all bets have been made on the final round of play. In high poker, the highest ranked hand wins the pot.

The other way is to force all the other players out of the game prior to the showdown, so that you are left alone in the game. At that point you can claim the pot and collect the winnings.

Forcing players out can be done by heavy betting, whether or not you have the hand to back up your betting. If you don't, that is known as **bluffing**—making it appear that you have a powerful hand by making big bets.

Study the rankings of the hands until you understand which hands are best, both in low and high poker. It's always amazing to see players who, after years of experience, still can't tell whether a flush or straight is a higher ranked hand.

The Deal

In all poker games, there must be someone to deal out the cards to the participants. In private games, one of the active players does this. Each player in a private game gets to deal, and the deal moves around the table in clockwise fashion.

In the casino games, the house employs a dealer who deals the cards all the time. The players never deal in a casino setting. In those games in which the dealer has an advantage by acting on his hand and betting last, such as **draw poker** and **hold 'em**, a button is moved around the table clockwise, so that each player in turn is the imaginary dealer when he has the **button**, and receives the advantages of playing and betting last.

The dealer has several obligations. He or she must shuffle the cards so that they are as random as possible when dealt out. The cards are usually given to the player to the dealer's right to be **cut**, that is, the top part removed and put to one side, after which the dealer restacks them with the bottom part of the deck now on top. In casino games, the dealer does this himself.

The dealer must then make sure that all antes are in the pot before dealing. He must make sure each player gets the required number of cards on each betting round, and that all bets are correct.

The dealer also calls the game, telling which player is to bet first on any particular round, and at the showdown, the dealer examines the players' hands to determine who has won the pot.

Antes

An ante may be called a sweetener. Each player, when an ante is required, places some money or chips in the center of the table prior to the first betting round. Usually it is a small percentage of the average bet, and is placed in the pot in order to force more action, since there will be more money to be won even on the first betting round.

In casino games there is usually an ante for every type of poker game. In private games, there is usually an ante only in the closed versions of poker such as draw poker.

Betting and Limits

Poker, after all, is a game played for money. Without money involved, it would be a dull game. All games have some kind of betting limit, which is usually two-tiered, such as $1-$2, or $5-$10 and so forth. Usually the higher limit is double the smaller one, but sometimes there is more of a spread, such as $1-$4.

A $1-$2 game means that all bets before the draw, including raises, are $1 and increments of $1; after the draw, $2 and increments of $2 are required when raising. There is betting on every round of play, and the higher limit prevails at certain times, as will be shown in the individual games.

In casino games, the limits will be shown for each table, usually by a sign above the individual poker table. If in doubt, ask the dealer. In private games, the betting limits are set by the players prior to play.

In private games, chips or money may be used. Chips are always preferable: they're easier to handle and to stack, and they come in different colors, to denote different denominations. Cash is always green, and it's cumbersome to place down and to stack.

In casino games, chips alone are used, except for coins. Usually the casino will use the same chips in general use for the other games. These chips usually come in $1, $5, $25 and $100 denominations. For antes and such, coins are used, usually 25¢ and 50¢ pieces.

When you go to a table in a casino, you will be required to get some chips. This is known as a **buy-in**, changing cash for chips. Usually there is a minimum amount you must buy-in for. The best rule is to have at least 40 times the minimum bet as your stake at the table. You don't have to have it all in cash. If you're at a $1-$4 table, for example, the buy-in required may only be $20. You can purchase $20 worth of chips and place $20 below that in cash on the table. That is your **table stake**. In casinos, you are playing table stakes. You can't take out more money from your pocket if you're involved in a game, and have to make a bet. However, you can always take out more money between deals and replenish your stake.

If you don't have enough table stake money to cover a larger bet, then you only participate in that part of the pot in which your money is already involved. The dealer will segregate subsequent bets into a different pot.

Betting Rounds

In the stud games, such as Seven-Card Stud and Hold 'em, there are a number of betting rounds. In draw poker, whether Jacks or Better, or Lowball, there are only two betting rounds, one before and one after the draw. All this will be explained in the individual games.

After all the betting is completed, if there are two or more players in the game, then there is a showdown. That's when the players show their hands to determine who is the winner. If one player shows the best hand, the others may concede the pot without showing theirs. If another player feels he has a stronger hand, though, then he or she shows the hand to claim the pot.

At the showdown, the player whose last bet or raise was called is the first to show his or her cards. Then the others in turn can show theirs.

Player's Options

Unless a bet is mandatory, as in the opening round of play, a player usually has a few options available to him. He may make the bet or he may **pass** or **check**. Passing or checking means not betting but having the option to see or call the other player's bet when it is his turn again.

Betting, like dealing, goes around the table in clockwise fashion. After a bet is made, the player whose turn it is can no longer pass or check and remain in the game. If he doesn't want to bet, he folds or discards his cards and is out of the game.

If he decides to stay in the game, however, he may call the previous bet by making a larger bet. For example, if the previous bet was $1, the player can raise by betting $2, the original call of $1, plus a $1 raise.

If the previous bet was a raise of another bet, then a player can reraise that raise. In casino games, there is usually a limit of three raises on any round of betting. If a player has previously checked his hand, he cannot raise when it is his turn to bet again, unless **check and raise** is allowed, where a raise is allowed after an initial *check*, which it usually is in casino play, but not in private games.

The Rake

In private games, no money is taken from the pot to run the game, but in the casino game, there is a **rake**, that is, money taken from each pot by the dealer, which is taken from the players and given to the house to run the game.

The rake varies from casino to casino. The smaller the game, the higher the percentage of the rake. Never play in a game with more than a 5% rake for the house. You'll be spinning your wheels in that game. Sometimes not only is there a limit on the percentage, but also the amount taken from each pot. For example, in some casinos where there's a 5% rake, no matter how big the pot is, no more than $2 or $2.50 may be taken out.

There's usually a sign near the table designating the rake. If in doubt, ask the dealer or the men who run the game in the casino. But you should know the rake before you sit down to play, and remember, make 5% the limit for yourself.

Seven-Card Stud

In stud poker, some of the cards are concealed, while others are seen by all the other players. In **seven-card stud**, there are three concealed cards, two dealt face down prior to the first betting round, and the final card dealt is face down, before the last betting round.

Seven-card stud is by far the most popular form of stud poker, and is one of the most popular poker games played privately in the Nevada casinos. As we discuss the game, we'll show the differences between the private and casino game, which, though minor, lead to somewhat different strategies at times.

The Fundamentals of Poker section should be consulted for the rank of cards and hands, object of the game and player's options, as well as the deal.

Play of the Game

In both the private and casino versions of the game, each player at the outset of play receives three cards from the dealer, dealt one at time, with the first two cards dealt face down and the third card dealt as an open card. Then the first round of betting commences.

In the private game, since this game provokes a lot of action, there's no ante. In the casino game, there's an ante, often 10% of the minimum bet. If it's a $5-$10 game, the ante is generally 50¢. In a smaller game, such as a $1-$4 game, the ante is either 10¢ or 25¢, but this ante structure varies in each casino.

The ante is put into the pot by all players prior to the deal. Thereafter it becomes part of the pot and goes to the winner of the pot.

After each player has his or her three cards, the first round of betting begins. There are altogether five rounds of betting in seven-card stud. The first round is usually called **Third Street** because three cards are already in each player's hand.

Seven Card Stud—Third Street

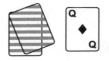

On Third Street in private games, the high card opens the betting. If two players have an equally high card, then the player closest to the dealer's left with the high card opens the betting. For purposes of betting, let's assume that all the games are $5-$10. The opening bet in a private game will be $5, and the high card holder must make this bet. It is mandatory.

Thereafter each player in turn, starting with the player to the opener's left, must either see, call, or raise the bet by making it $10.

If a player doesn't want to bet on this opening round of play, he is out of the game, and his cards are folded and handed to the dealer, who puts them to one side, out of play.

Let's see this in illustrative form. We'll assume there are eight players at the table in a private game. Player A is the opener. ** stands for the **hole cards** (those that are face-down).

Player A. **K	**Player E.** **Q
Player B. **3	**Player F.** **5
Player C. **10	**Player G.** **9
Player D. **4	**Player H.** **8

Player A puts $5 into the pot. Player B folds by turning over his 3 and giving the dealer his three cards. Player C folds, Player D calls with a $5 bet. Players E, F and G also fold. Player H raises the bet to $10.

Now only Players A and H are in the game. It's now up to Player A. He can call the raise by betting an additional $5, go out, or reraise. Let's suppose he reraises, moving the bet up to $15 by putting in an additional $10 (he already had bet $5). Now Player D has to bet an additional $10 to stay in the game. He makes the $10 bet and Player H adds another $5 to his bet to call Player A's reraise, and they're all in for the next round of betting.

The dealer now gives each player another open card. Player A is closest to the dealer's left and gets the first card. On this round the hands look like this.

Player A. **K Q
Player D. **4 4
Player H. **8 J

The highest hand now belongs to Player D. In stud poker, when there are two levels of betting as here ($5-$10) a player can open with a $10 bet only when there is an open pair showing, or on *Fifth Street*, even if there isn't an open pair. This round of play is *Fourth Street*.

On the second round of betting and on all subsequent rounds, the player with the high hand can either check his hand or make a bet. If he checks, he must call a bet or raise to stay in the game, but he can't raise after checking in a private game.

Here Player D checks, and Player H bets $10. Player A raises the bet to $20, and Player D calls the bet, but Player H now folds his cards, leaving only Players A and D in the game. There will be three more betting rounds, with the last betting round coming after they've each received a facedown card. Let's suppose it's now *Seventh Street*, the final betting round, and this is the situation.

Player A. **K Q 5 9 *
Player D. **4 4 3 A *

Player D is still high with his 4s. He bets $10 and Player A calls the bet. Now we have the showdown, since all the betting rounds are over. Both players will show their cards and the best hand wins the pot.

Player D, who was called, must show his cards first. He has 4 K 4 4 3 A J. Selecting five of those cards to form his best hand, it is 444 AK, Three-of-a-Kind.

WINNING POKER

Player A shows his hand, Q J K Q 5 9 10. His best hand is K Q J 10 9, a Straight. Since a Straight beats a Three-of-a-Kind, Player A wins the pot. If he had a weaker hand than Player D, he'd have the option of not showing his hand, by just conceding the pot to Player D.

We see now that in seven-card stud, we use the seven cards dealt to us to form our best hand of five cards.

What we've just discussed is the private game. In the casino game there is a fixed dealer, who always deals the cards, and he or she is a house employee.

In all games played in a casino, expect to have a rake. Usually the rake is about 5%. Sometimes it's more, very rarely less. In a number of games, although there might be a rake of 5%, there's also a limit of $1, $2, or $2.50 that will be taken out of the pot no matter how big the pot is.

In casino games, expect also to ante. We'll discuss the basic $5-$10 seven-card stud game here. The ante is 50¢ and the rake is 5% or $2.50, whichever is less.

All players ante before the deal. With eight players in the game, the ante comes to $4, money that is often fought for immediately with raises on the opening round.

In the casino game, the low card opens. This makes for more action, and the more bets there are, the more money the casino makes. Also, the game becomes a livelier and better game. A $5-$10 bet is usually much more conservative in a casino than in a private game.

Instead of low card betting $5, in the casino game, he can bet $1, but he must make his bet. Then he can be raised to $4, and thereafter the raises will be in $5 increments on the opening round, Third Street. On the other rounds, the betting will be $5 unless it's Fifth Street or an open pair shows, when the betting will be at a $10 level with increments of $10.

On the opening round, if two players have the same ranked low card, since the dealer is in a stationary spot, the player with the lower ranked suit opens. For purposes of opening on this round, and this round only, the suits, in descending order, are ranked, spades, hearts, diamonds and clubs.

I will illustrate a game.

Player A.	**9	**Player E.**	**A
Player B.	**Q	**Player F.**	**J
Player C.	**3	**Player G.**	**4
Player D.	**5	**Player H.**	**K

Player C must open with a $1 bet. His 3 is the low card on board. Player D, next in turn, folds. Player E raises to $4. Players F and G fold. Player H calls the $4 bet. Player A folds and Player B raises to $9 with an increment of $5 over the previous raise.

Now it's up to Player C, who folds. Player E calls by putting in $5 more. Player H calls.

We now have Players B, E and H in the game. They each get another card on Fourth Street, and this is how their hands look.

> **Player B.** **Q A
> **Player E.** **A 9
> **Player H.** **K 2

Player B is high with A Q. He bets $5 and players E and H call. On Fifth Street the hands look like this.

> **Player B.** **Q A 6
> **Player E.** **A 9 4
> **Player H.** **K 2 K

Player H is now high with his Ks, and he bets $10. Player B calls and Player E folds.

On Sixth Street the hands look like this.

> **Player B.** **Q A 6 3
> **Player H.** **K 2 K Q

Player H is still high and bets $10. Player B folds, leaving Player H alone in the game. He wins the pot, but doesn't have to show his hole cards. The game is over and the players ante before a new game is dealt.

Strategy at Seven-Card Stud

The first and most important strategy is what to stay in with on Third Street. Only stay in with Three-of-a-Kind, a Three Flush, a Three Straight, a high pair (10s or higher), or a lower pair with an A, K or Q as odd card.

Don't stay in with any other hands. You might also stay in with a small pair, lower than a 10, if both are concealed, no matter what the odd card. But that's it.

On Fourth Street, if your Three Flush or Three Straight doesn't improve, get out of the game. Fold your cards. If a bigger pair shows than your pair, unless your odd card is higher than the pair showing, go out also. Don't stay in with second-rate cards. Only the best hand wins, not second or third best.

How to bet your cards? With Three-of-a-Kind, play them slow. Don't raise until Fifth Street. With a high pair (10s or higher) come out rising, unless you see someone else has a higher pair. In that case, fold them. With a small pair and a high **kicker**, or odd card, call and try to improve on Fourth Street. If you don't improve and face higher pairs, go out.

With a possible Flush or Straight, even if you improve to a Four Flush or Four Straight on Fourth Street, you're still an underdog against a pair of Ks. These are known as drawing cards (the four Straights and Flushes) and you call until you have made your hand, then raise.

That's the basic strategy. You want to have a possible winning hand by the showdown. If you're beaten on board, don't chase the other player. Only when your hand is strong and can get strong enough to win do you stay in. With good cards, play aggressively. With drawing cards play conservatively within the boundaries of the strategies mentioned above.

One final note: in the private games, once a player has checked, he can't raise. In the casino games, "check and raise" is permitted. It is useful on rare occasions, and shouldn't be used until you're an expert in the game, but be aware that it is the casino rule.

Texas Hold 'em

Hold 'em, as the game is also called, is one of the most popular and fastest growing games being played today, and can be found in many casinos, especially in Las Vegas. The game is usually played with eleven participants, and is a high action money game.

Play of the Game

In casino games, there's only one dealer, and there's usually an ante, though it can be rather small (less than 10%) of the minimum bet. Since the dealer is stationary throughout play, a button is moved around the table after each deal, and the person who has the *button* is the imaginary dealer, with the player to his or her left having to make the first bet.

A button is used because position is important in this game, and it is to a player's benefit to bet in a late position, seeing what the other players have done first before committing himself.

In this game, there's usually a **blind**. A **blind bettor** must make a bet on the opening round of play, regardless of the value of his cards. This is done to promote action, and make the game livelier.

Usually the blind bet is less than the customary wager. For example, in a $5-$10 game, the blind bettor must open for $1 or $2. He can then be raised to $4 (sometimes $5). Thereafter the betting is at the lower range of the game, $5 until a later round of betting. Rules of betting vary from game to game and casino to casino. Check with the dealer when in doubt about the betting or about any other rules.

The dealer deals out two cards to each player, both cards face down, and dealt one at a time. The first player to receive a card is the one to the left of the button; the last player to get his card is the button.

After each player has received his or her two cards there is a betting round. Here the blind bettor opens, and then the betting goes around in turn, with each player having the opportunity to call the bet, raise it or go out by folding his cards. No player can check on this round.

After all bets have been made, the dealer will turn up three cards on board. These are community cards, used by all the players equally to form their best hands. Altogether there will be five cards on board, but the players will only receive their original two closed cards, no more.

Hold 'em—The Flop

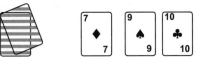

The three cards dealt face up on board are known as the **flop**. Altogether five cards will be on board, and the players will use three of these, combined with their own two cards, to form their best high poker hand, for Hold 'Em is a game of high poker.

After the flop, the betting continues for another round. Here, the first player to bet is the blind. If he's folded, the player still in the game who's closest to the left of the button bets. Then the betting goes around in clockwise fashion, with any player able to open the betting. If it's a $5-$10 game, the opening bet must be $5. After the bet has been opened, any player may call, or raise or fold. Raises are in $5 increments.

Then there's another card put out on board. Now we have another betting round, called Fourth Street, with the bets now moving into the higher range; $10 in a $5-$10 game. After this round, another card is dealt face up on board, and now we have the final betting round, known as Fifth Street.

After all bets are made on this round, and if there are two or more players remaining in the game, there's a showdown, with the highest hand winning the pot.

Strategy at Hold 'em

There are two aspects to strategy at Hold 'em. The first is the cards to stay in with, and the second is the position you're in at the table. Let's now examine the best cards to stay in with. There are really three groups: the very best, strong, and marginal hands.

In Hold 'em you're going to get only two cards at the outset, and then you're going to have to eventually share all the board's cards with other players at the table. If you improve, they may also improve. So, from the outset, you want to have the kind of hands that can win at the showdown, when all the bets have been made and the players show their hands to determine the winner of the pot.

Very Best Hands

These are the best possible hands to hold prior to the flop, in descending order. When we speak of *suited* we mean both cards are of the same suit.

A A
K K
A K (suited)
Q Q
A Q (suited)

With these cards you're going to be aggressively raising no matter what position you're in, right from the beginning. It may turn out that even these powerful hands will be weakened when the flop comes out, but unless the flop contains a Four Flush or Four Straight in which you have no involvement, or shows Three-of-a-Kind, where the fourth card may be held by one of the other players still in the game, you want to raise and force the other player to submit to your bets in the hope that they won't draw out on you, that is, draw cards that will beat your hand.

Strong Hands

We'll look at these in descending order.

A K (not suited)

A Q (not suited)

A J (not suited)

A 10 (suited)

K Q (suited)

Why are the A hands so strong? Because a pair of As is generally boss in Hold 'em. Suppose you hold K Q of diamonds and the flop comes up 9 of spades, 6 of diamonds and a 4 of clubs. At this point you're not even the favorite. One of the players against you probably has an A in his hand. Perhaps two players hold an A.

If Fourth Street comes up with any card but a diamond, K or Q, you're dead. You have to pray for a K or Q on Fifth Street. If you don't get it, forget about these cards. Even a flop of K of spades, 10 of clubs, 5 of hearts followed by Fourth Street of 2 of diamonds and Fifth Street of A of clubs buries you. That A is a *scare card*, and you can figure that at this moment someone has combined for at least two As with an A in his or her hand.

Marginal Hands

These are listed in descending order.

J J

10 10

A J (not suited)

A 10 (not suited)

K J (suited)

9 9

8 8

Q J (suited)

J 10 (suited)

With these cards, you have to be careful, hoping to stay in cheaply for the flop, so that you can draw cards to improve your hand. Suppose you stay in with K J suited in clubs, and the flop comes up A of spades, 4 of diamonds and 3 of hearts.

At this point, you have to expect another player to have at least a pair of As. You are dead here and must throw away your cards.

This leads to another principle of Hold 'em. Try and get your big bets in before the draw if you have the very best cards, to prevent the strong and marginal hands from hanging around to see the flop.

The next most important consideration is position. The earlier you have to bet or act on your hand, the weaker your position. The later, the stronger your position.

Take advantage of position by betting aggressively with strong hands or by staying in cheaply with marginal hands. The better your position, the easier it is to stay in for the flop.

For example, if you hold J J, a marginal hand at best, and you're in 10th position at the table, your position is great. If there have been a few raises to you, throw away the cards. If you are able to get in cheaply, by all means do so. If you're in early position, let's say 3rd, and you call the opener, if there are a few raises behind you, don't stay in. You're facing big hands, and if any scare card comes out, which for you is a Q K or A, you know you're a heavy underdog with your Js.

Also, gauge your opponents, and find out who stays in with weak hands and who plays tight. This, together with position and good cards, will make you a winner.

Draw Poker—Jacks or Better

This is a closed variation of high poker, also called **Jackpots**. By closed, we mean that all the player's cards are unseen by the other participants, whereas, in stud poker, some of the cards are seen by all players. In Hold 'em, the player has two **pocket**, or closed cards, but all the community cards are exposed. In draw poker, however, they're all hidden.

Play of the Game

There is usually an ante, whether this game is played at home, in a casino, or a club, since draw poker is legal in the California clubs. The ante is usually about 10% of the maximum bet, which in a $5-$10 game, would be $1. Antes vary from game to game and casino to casino, however.

The best game is with eight players, and each player gets to deal in a private game. The dealer has an advantage, for he or she gets to bet and act last. Position is of great importance in draw poker.

In the casino games, where there is a stationary dealer, a button is moved around the table clockwise, so that each player, in turn, gets the button and is the imaginary dealer.

Each player is dealt five cards face down, one card at a time, after all the antes are in the pot. The player to the left of the dealer or button is the first to act.

In draw poker, there will be two betting rounds: one before the draw and one after it. The draw, as we shall see, allows players to discard cards from their hands and get new ones from the dealer in an attempt to improve their holdings.

In the game of Jacks or better, a player can only open the betting if his hand contains at least a pair of Js, or a higher ranked pair or a higher ranked holding. Thus, a pair of 10s can't open the betting, but Qs can. Any stronger hand than a pair of Js, such as a Three-of-a-Kind, a Straight, and so forth, can also open the betting.

If a player's hand is weaker than Js, he must check on the opening round. The players in turn may check until one player can open the betting. After the opener has bet, then each player, starting with the player to the opener's left, can fold and go out, call the bet, or raise.

Let's follow a game to see how it's done.

Player A. Q J 7 6 4	**Player E.** A J J 4 2	
Player B. A 7 5 4 2	**Player F.** 3 3 3 9 6	
Player C. J 10 9 8 4	**Player G.** Q 10 6 5 2	
Player D. K K 8 5 2	**Dealer** 7 7 A 6 3	

Players A, B and C must check, since they don't have openers. Player D opens the betting with $5. Player E folds. Though he has Js, he knows they have little value, since Player D had to have Js or better. Player F raises to $10. Player G and the dealer fold. Players A and B fold, and Player C, who has a Four-Straight, calls the $10 bet. Player D puts in $5 more to call Player F's raise.

Now there are three players remaining in the game, C, D and F. At this point, there is a draw. Each player in turn, starting with Player C, the player closest to the dealer's left, may draw as many cards as he wishes to improve his hand. He draws one, throwing away the 4 face down, and is given one card by the dealer. Player D throws away three cards, retaining the Ks, and is dealt three cards face down by the dealer. Player F draws two cards, retaining his three 3s, and gets two cards face down from the dealer. Now there is another betting round.

At this point, let's see how the hands look.

Player C. J 10 9 8 9
Player D. K K 8 8 10
Player F. 3 3 3 K 7

The opener is first to bet in the second

round. Player D checks. He may do this and still come into the betting later. Player F bets $10, the higher range of the $5-$10 game, which comes into effect after the draw. Player C, who didn't get his straight, folds. Player D, with two pair, is afraid Player F is bluffing, so he calls the $10 bet.

Now all betting rounds are finished. Player F, who is called, shows his three 3s. Player D concedes without showing his cards, for he is beaten. He may do this. If he had stronger cards than Player F, he would have shown them to claim the pot. But Player F wins the pot.

Strategy in Draw Poker—Jacks or Better

As with most poker games, the most important strategy is knowing what cards to stay in with, and what hands to fold at the outset.

Even though any hand of Js or better may open, draw poker is a game of position. Depending upon your position, you open with varying hands. For example, if we were to divide position into early, middle and late, with the first three players having early position, the next three middle and the last two late position, we can see that opening with a pair of Js in early position is a very weak play.

If any other player stays in and raises, the holder of the Js would know he is already beaten, and is an underdog to win the pot. The following are guides for opening the pot.

In early position, don't open with less than As.

In middle position, don't open with less than Ks.

In late position you can open with Js.

The above rules are for very tight players. When there is a larger ante, more than 10% of the highest possible bet, then you can loosen up a little. With a higher ante structure:

• In early position, you can open with Ks.
• In middle position, you can open with Qs.
• In late position, you can open with Js.

When you have two small pairs (10s or smaller) you shouldn't open in early position, and don't even call with them if there are three other players who have already bet. The odds against improving two pairs are 11-1, and you're probably already beaten.

If you hold a pair of Ks or As and are in late position, with only the opener, you can raise with these cards.

With Four Straights and Four Flushes, don't raise. You have to draw to win, and the odds are approximately 4-1 against your improving your hand.

Study your opposition. See who plays tight and who is weak, and adjust your strategy accordingly. Against tight players, play very conservatively. With weak players, you can be more aggressive and play slightly weaker hands.

Draw Poker—Lowball

This is the most popular version of low poker and is sometimes spelled **loball**. It's played at home, in casinos and in the California poker clubs.

Lowball poker is just the opposite of high poker. In this variation of the game, the low hand wins, not the high hand.

The lowest (and best) hand in lowball is 5 4 3 2 A, which is knows as a **wheel** or **bicycle**. The next best hand is a 6 4 3 2 A, then a 6 5 3 2 A, then a 6 5 4 2 A, and so forth, each hand a little higher than the other.

Lowball—The Wheel

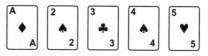

In low poker straights and flushes don't count. You don't have to pay attention to the suits or to the fact that cards may be in consecutive order. What is important is the relative rank of the cards. The most important card in low poker, as it is in high poker, is the A. But in lowball, it counts as 1 and is always the lowest card in any hand of lowball.

When announcing your holding in low poker, the custom is to call out the two highest cards. For instance, if you held 8 5 4 3 A, you'd call out, "I have an 8 5."

The hands just shown, the wheel and the 6-high hands are really and truly the best hands in lowball. Any 7-high hand is very strong. As we get to the 8-high and hands headed by even higher cards, they lose strength. Remember, any hand of five odd cards will beat any hand containing one pair, because this is the reverse of high poker.

Play of the Game

This game is sometimes played with a joker, known as a **bug**. When used in lowball, it can stand for any card the player wants. For example, if a player held 7 5 4 3 and a Joker, he'd value the Joker as an A, or 1.

However, many games played at home and in casinos don't have a joker, so we're going to discuss the game without the joker, just using the standard 52-card pack of cards.

There is usually an ante in lowball draw unless there is a blind bettor. Sometimes there is an ante and a blind bettor. For purposes of illustration, let's assume we're playing a $3-$5 game without an ante, but with a blind bettor at a casino in Las Vegas.

To remind you, a $3-$5 game means that all bets before the draw, including raises, are $3 and increments of $3; after the draw, bets are $5 and increments of $5 when raising.

Each player will receive five cards dealt face down one at a time by the dealer, beginning with the player to the button's left and going around the table clockwise. In draw poker, all cards are closed, none of the players see any of the other participants' cards.

After each player has five cards, the player to the button's left, being designated as the blind, must make a bet on this round of play, no matter what the value of his hand.

He bets $3. Now, each player in turn, beginning with the blind's left all the way around to the button, must either call, raise or fold his cards. No one can check on this round of play. Let's follow a game to see how it works.

Blind	K K Q Q J	**Player D.** 8 6 5 3 A
Player A.	J 9 9 8 5	**Player E.** K 4 3 2 A
Player B.	10 7 5 4 4	**Player F.** J 10 10 9 8
Player C.	7 6 5 4 Q	**Button** Q 7 7 6 A

The blind must bet $3. Player A and B fold. Player C calls the bet, Player D, with an "8 6 high" raises to $6. Player E calls the raise, Player F and the button fold. The blind now folds, and Player C calls the raise by putting in $3 more.

Now the first round of betting is over. Players C, D and E remain in the game. Player C will draw first. He takes one card, discarding his Q. Player D stands **pat**, drawing no cards, satisfied with his hand. Player E draws one card, discarding the K.

Now it's up to Player C to go first. He can check on this round and still remain in the game. Here's how the hands now look after the draw.

Player C. 7 6 5 4 J
Player D. 8 6 5 3 A
Player E. 8 4 3 2 A

Player C, whose hand is now pretty bad, checks. Player D bets $5 and Player E raises to $10. Player C folds his cards, and Player D calls the raise by putting in $5 more.

All the bets have been made and now we have the showdown. Player E, whose raise was called, shows his "8 4 high." Player D, who has an "8 6 high," concedes the pot to Player

E, who wins all the money.

Player E is said to have a **smooth** 8, while Player D had a **rough** 8 high hand. A smooth hand is one where the rest of the cards are very low; a rough one is where they are rather high.

After this game is over, the button will be moved so that the former blind is now the button, while the player to his left, Player A, will now become the blind.

Strategy at Draw Poker—Lowball

As with most other poker games, the important considerations are the cards to stay in with, and your position at the table.

If you're the blind, you must stay in with any hand, because you have already bet, and if there are no raises on the first round, you can draw up to five cards to improve your hand. After all, you have nothing to lose.

Should there be a raise, your cards become hopeless. Then you fold them, kissing good-bye to the bet you made. Other players will be the blind in turn, and you should assume that a blind bet is no more than a forced ante.

Now, let's go into strategy. You should never stay in the game if you have to draw more than one card. That's the limit. With two cards to draw, you are a terrible underdog, and will be a loser in the long run. The way to spot a weak player is to see how many cards he draws. If he draws two, he has little strength.

A pat hand is a hand that will stand by itself without drawing another card to it, and one should never stay in with pat hands headed by Js, Qs or Ks. They're losers. Only in very late position, being the button or next to it, should we hazard a 10-high pat hand, and only to see the blind, without other players in the game.

With a pat hand, you can open (or see the blind bet) with an 8-high hand in the first three positions. In the next three positions you can do the same with a 9-high hand, and only in the last two positions should you do so with a 10-high hand.

When you have a drawing hand, that is, a hand that needs one card to improve it, then your hand has to be a little stronger to justify opening. In the first three positions at the table, you won't see the blind's bet or open the betting if there's no blind, unless you have a four-card holding of a 7 or less. In the next three positions, an 8-high drawing hand is okay, and in the last two positions, a 9-high drawing hand is sufficient.

When you have pat hands, you can play them more aggressively. With a 7-high pat hand, you can raise the blind from any position, but with an 8-high pat hand, you can raise from only the last three positions at the table. A 9-high pat hand should be raised against a blind for the last three positions also, but if there has been another player in the game, just call.

To clarify position once more, the blind is the first position, the button is the last position. The player to the left of the blind is position 2; the player to his left is position 3, and so forth. Thus, in our illustrative game, Player A was in position 2, while Player F was in seventh position.

When a blind is in the game, and you're in late position with an opening hand and there are no other players in the game, you want to raise more aggressively, to force out the blind and win his bet.

Don't let the blind stay in to draw cards if you can help it. Get him out, and try to grab his bet if you're in there alone with him.

Glossary of Poker Terms

Ace—The most valuable card in poker; of highest rank in high poker, and valued as a 1 in lowball.

Ante—Money or chips placed into the pot by players before the first betting round.

Bet—Money or chips placed into the pot by players on any betting round.

Betting Round—A round of play in which bets are made.

Bicycle—The best and lowest in lowball, consisting of 5 4 3 2 A, also called a **Wheel**.

Blind, Blind Opener—The player to the left of the dealer or button who must make a bet on the first betting round.

Bluffing—Betting heavily on a poor hand to give the impression that it has great value.

Board—Cards which are seen by all the players, as in Hold 'em.

Bug—A wild card in lowball, which can be used by its holder as any card. Also known as **Joker**.

Button—An object resembling a button which is moved around the table clockwise to denote an imaginary dealer.

Buy—See **Draw a Card**.

Buy-In—Money changed into chips prior to play in a casino game.

Call, Call A Bet—Making a bet equal to the previous bet or raise. Also known as **Seeing a Bet**.

Check—Passing the opportunity to bet. Also known as **Pass**.

Check and Raise—Being able to raise after first checking.

Community Cards—In Hold 'em, cards which can be used by all players to make their best hand.

Deuce—The poker term for the 2.

Draw—The taking of additional cards prior to the second round of betting in draw poker.

Draw a Card—Getting another card prior to any betting round. Also known as **Buy**.

Draw Poker—The closed version of poker.

Flop—The first three open community cards dealt out at one time in Hold'em.

Flush—A hand which contains five cards of the same suit.

Fold—To throw away or discard one's cards during any betting round.

Four Flush—Having four cards of the same suit.

Four-of-a-Kind—A hand consisting of four cards of the same rank such as 8 8 8 8.

Four Straight—Four cards to a Straight.

Full House—A holding of Three-of-a-Kind plus a pair.

Hand—The five cards a player holds, or the best five cards of his holding which make up his strongest hand.

High Poker—The form of poker in which the highest hand wins.

Hole Card—A card held by the player which is unseen by other players.

Jacks or Better, Jackpots—High draw poker where a holding of at least a pair of Js is necessary to open the betting.

Joker—See **Bug**.

Kicker—An odd high card, usually an A.

Lowball—A poker game in which the low hand wins the pot.

Opener—The player who makes the first bet on any betting round.

Openers—In Jacks or Better, holding at least the pair of Js after making the first bet.

Pair—Two cards of the same rank.

Pass—See **Check**.

Pat Hand—A hand in draw poker which doesn't need another card drawn to it.

Pot—The amount of money and antes already bet by the player; this amount goes to the winner.

Raise—A bet which is higher than the previous bet.

Rake—The casino's cut of money taken from the pot.

Reraise—Making a higher bet than a previous raise.

Rough—In lowball, having high cards which form a hand. For example 9 8 7 5 4 is a rough 9.

See a Bet—See **Call**.

Showdown—Showing of hands after the last

bet to determine who is the winner of the pot.

Smooth—In lowball, low cards after the highest card. 9 5 4 3 2 a is a smooth 9.

Straight—A high poker hand containing five cards of consecutive rank, such as Q J 10 9 8.

Straight Flush—Five cards in sequence and of the same suit, such as ♦Q ♦J ♦10 ♦9♦ 8.

Stud Poker—The form of poker where one or more of the player's cards are seen by other players.

Three-of-a-Kind—A hand consisting of three cards of the same rank, such as 5 5 5.

Two Pair—A hand consisting of two sets of cards of the same rank, such as K K and 4 4.

Wheel—See **Bicycle**.

Wild Card—A card which can be made into any card desired to form the best possible hand.

Winning Keno

Introduction

Keno is one of the most popular of the casino games in Nevada, and millions play it every year. The game is fast moving, and for a little bit of money, you can win a great deal, up to $50,000. To win this amount, all that is required is luck and a relatively small bet.

This huge payoff for a small wager makes Keno a very attractive game. You can play the game while in a casino restaurant or while waiting for someone to show up for an appointment. I know of a lucky man who won $12,000 while waiting for his wife to come out of the women's room.

That's the kind of game keno is. Lightning can strike at any moment, and you might be the lucky winner of $50,000.

History of Keno

Keno is one of the most ancient of games, and as its name implies, its origins are Oriental. It was invented about two thousand years ago, during the Han Dynasty of China, by Cheung Leung, in order to raise money for the army.

It was a great success, and its popularity has gone on unabated to the present day. Of course, during that long period of time, it underwent a number of changes. Originally it was played in Chinese and contained 120 Chinese characters, drawn from the **Thousand Character Book**, which was written by that great sage, Confucius, and his followers. This work is a classic, and literate Chinese know and study it.

The number of characters was slowly reduced to 90 while the game was played in China, and then, with the great emigrations of Chinese to America, the game was imported, and the characters reduced even further to 80. Today keno is played with the same 80 possibilities, though now the characters have been changed to numbers for simplicity.

Just before the turn of the 20th Century, the game was very popular among the Chinese who had settled in several of the big American cities, particularly in San Francisco.

WINNING KENO

It was an illegal game, but it was so popular among the Chinese that this didn't seem to matter. It kept growing in popularity.

At this time, the usual ticket was what we'd term a **ten-spot**, that is, ten numbers were selected by the player, and the payoffs were as listed below. **Catch** refers to the number of characters that were selected by the operator matching the number of characters picked by the players.

19th Century Keno Payoffs	
Catch	**Payoff**
5	2 for 1
6	20 for 1
7	200 for 1
8	1000 for 1
9	1500 for 1
10	3000 for 1

Note the term *2 for 1*, which is the payoff for 5 catches. If you bet $1, you'd get only $2 back—your dollar plus a dollar profit. When a payoff is at *2 to 1*, you'd get back your dollar plus two additional dollars.

The game was in the form of a lottery, and the big payoffs possible interested not only the Chinese, but also Americans who wanted to take a chance and, in those non-inflationary days, risk a nickel or a dime to pick up some good money. For Americans who couldn't read Chinese, this presented all kinds of difficulties, because it was practically impossible to figure out which characters had caught.

The operators of the game had a big advantage over the players, particularly in the larger payoffs, and so to get Americans to play keno, the game changed from Chinese characters to ordinary numbers, keeping the same format of 80. At this point, the keno houses had tickets marked from 1-80, and the numbers, familiar to Americans, could be easily understood.

In those early days, the numbers were printed on wooden balls and moved around by hand. They were then randomly put through a **goose**, a long tube similar to the goose used in keno lounges today. Since hands touched the balls, though, there was a chance of fixed games. Today, the casinos use air to move ping pong balls imprinted with numbers around as randomly as possible, and then the balls are forced into a goose one by one without anyone touching them. This method makes for an honest game and gives all players the same equal chance to win.

Because the Nevada Gambling Act of 1931, which legalized gambling in the Silver State, expressly forbade lotteries, the casinos

introduced the game as *Race Horse Keno*.
There were still problems, and the race horse
aspect of keno was dropped when the U.S.
Government passed a law taxing off-track betting. After that the game was known as just
plain keno.

The game has grown in popularity year
by year, and many old-timers in Las Vegas
bemoan the loss of cocktail and entertainment
lounges as they've turned into keno lounges.
Time marches on, though, and the public's
infatuation with keno had to be recognized and
serviced.

Inflation has played a role in the game. In
1963, the payout limit was $25,000. That limit
was maintained for a number of years, until in
1979 it was raised to $50,000. The ticket price
has also gone up steadily. **Straight tickets**
have gone from 60¢ to 70¢, though today it's
hard to buy a keno ticket, particularly on the
Las Vegas Strip, for less than $1.

Keno Lounge and Employees

The area in which keno is played is called
the **keno lounge**. It consists of a keno counter,
behind which sit **keno writers**, who receive
the tickets played by the bettors, mark them,
and collect money for the game.

In some instances, bettors' tickets are brought to this area by **keno runners**. These house employees, usually women, pick up tickets from people who want to play the next game, but can't get to the keno lounge. This group includes bettors at table games, diners in the various restaurants, and people in other parts of the casino. In this way, through the use of keno runners, players in a casino, no matter where they are, can usually play keno without having to go to the keno lounge.

Not only do the keno writers collect bets, they also make the payoffs on winning tickets. Behind the keno writers is the operator who calls the game. He sits on an elevated seat and starts the game by pressing a button, which automatically mixes the ping pong balls. They are in a large, transparent bowl, and they're stirred randomly by the air forced into the bowl, which in turn forces the balls, one by one, into one of two transparent gooses (the long tubes), each of which hold ten balls.

After the game begins, the operator calls each number aloud as it is pushed into a goose. That number is then marked electrically on a **keno board**. This board holds all eighty numbers, and each number lights up as it is called. After twenty numbers have been called, the game is over. From these twenty numbers, each player will examine his or her tickets to see if he has *caught* enough numbers to collect some money.

Keno boards are located throughout the casino and adjacent areas, such as restaurants and coffee shops, so that players, no matter where they are when playing the game, can see if they won or lost.

The keno lounge is made up of rows of seats, each with an armrest. On each armrest is a box holding the crayons and keno blanks, which are used to play the game.

While in the keno lounge, a player can order beverages from waitresses who constantly service the area. These drinks are free for active keno players, who usually tip, or toke, the waitresses when they receive their complimentary drink.

How to Play Keno

Let's assume you're at the keno lounge and want to play a game. The first thing you'll notice is that the board will be lit by twenty numbers from the previous game. At the bottom of the board there will be another figure, indicating the number of the previous game. For example, if the bottom number is 236, game 236 has just been played, and the next game will be game 237. The number will be changed to 237 when all twenty numbers have been turned off, indicating that a new sequence of numbers is about to be called for game 237. Once the board is empty of printed numbers, it's too late to make a keno bet. The next game is already on.

While the board is filled with twenty lit numbers, bets can be made for the next game. To place a bet, the player must first pick up a blank ticket, also known as a **blank**, and fill it in. He or she should "X" **out** not only the numbers he selects, which may be from one to fifteen **spots**, but also the amount to be bet and the number of spots selected. Let's first look at a keno blank.

Keno Blank

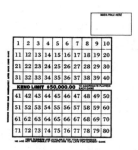

This blank is from a very popular gambling casino in downtown Las Vegas. Between the top and bottom rows of numbers is the statement *KENO LIMIT $50,000.00 to aggregate players each game*.

This statement means that the most the casino will pay out for any game of keno is $50,000. In the unlikely event that two players will each be entitled to $50,000 for one game's payoff, each one will get $25,000. That's the rule because of the gambling commission laws. Don't worry about that, though, because it's very unlikely that anyone will win $50,000.00, let alone two players winning that amount and having to split it.

Next, notice that there's a rectangular box in the upper right hand corner marked *Mark Price Here*. The player should put in that box the amount he wants to bet. If it's $1, then write 1 in the box. Leave out the dollar ($) or cents (¢) sign.

To the right of the numbers is another long blank space. In this space, the bettor should put the total spots selected. If two numbers are selected, the ticket is known as a **two-spot** ticket. A player can select up to fifteen spots on a straight ticket.

The numbers selected should be "X"ed out using the crayon the casino has available to all keno bettors. After you've Xed out the numbers, add up the spots selected, and put this number to the right of the ticket. Then put the amount you wish to bet in the price box, on the right hand top corner of the ticket.

When that's done, bring the ticket to the keno writer. If you're in the keno lounge, you can go directly to the keno writer. If you're not in the lounge, you'd give the keno ticket and the bet to a runner.

The following is a filled-in ticket. It is known as an **original** or **master** ticket. It is a **five-spot straight ticket**, since five numbers were selected, and it is being played for $1.

Five-Spot Original Ticket

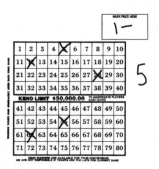

With this ticket in hand, you go to the keno writer and pay him or her a dollar to play the next game. He or she will retain the master and give you back a **duplicate** ticket, which you hold on to till the game is over. A duplicate ticket of the original we showed will look like this:

WINNING KENO

Five-Spot Duplicate Ticket

This duplicate shows a few things that weren't on the original blank. There's the date and time the ticket was played, and the game number, which is 289. There's also another code number. All of these are printed on duplicates to prevent collusion and cheating and to protect the players and the casino.

Note also the lettering on the right side of the ticket. Reading down, this message says *Winning tickets must be paid immediately after each keno game*. If you're entitled to a payoff, you *must* present your duplicate ticket to the writer or runner before the next game is called. Otherwise you'll forfeit your winnings. This rule is in effect to prevent the keno game from being called a lottery, where winning tickets can be collected at any time. It's very important. Don't forget to collect your winnings before the next game is called, or you won't collect anything.

The ticket just played is known as a **five-spot**, since five numbers were selected. It's a **straight ticket** because it was played only one way, and if enough numbers were called by the operator there would be a payoff.

In order to collect and win with this five-spot ticket, at least three numbers would have to catch. The payoff possibilities at this down-town casino are as follows:

A Five-Spot Payoff	
Winning Spots	**Payoff**
3	$1.00
4	$14.00
5	$720.00

That's for a $1 ticket. If the player played a $2 ticket, the payoffs would be exactly double, and for a $5 ticket, they'd be five times the $1 payoff. The player doesn't get better odds playing for more money; all he does is risk more to collect more.

How does the player know how much he will collect and how many numbers he must catch to win some money? There are small booklets available at each seat in the keno lounge and at each table in the casino restaurant which show the payoffs and the bets allowed. These are also known as **rate cards**.

A sample rate card, showing all payoffs and bets available, as well as the total numbers one must catch to win anything, is shown below.

Rate Card

MARK 1 SPOT

Winning Spots	$1.00 Ticket Pays	$3.00 Ticket Pays	$5.00 Ticket Pays	$1.40 Ticket Pays
1	3.00	9.00	15.00	4.20

MARK 2 SPOTS

Winning Spots	$1.00 Ticket Pays	$3.00 Ticket Pays	$5.00 Ticket Pays	$1.40 Ticket Pays
2	12.00	36.00	60.00	17.00

MARK 3 SPOTS

Winning Spots	$1.00 Ticket Pays	$3.00 Ticket Pays	$5.00 Ticket Pays	$1.40 Ticket Pays
2	1.00	3.00	5.00	1.40
3	42.00	126.00	210.00	60.00

MARK 4 SPOTS

Winning Spots	$1.00 Ticket Pays	$3.00 Ticket Pays	$5.00 Ticket Pays	$1.40 Ticket Pays
2	1.00	3.00	5.00	1.40
3	4.00	12.00	20.00	5.60
4	112.00	336.00	560.00	160.00

MARK 5 SPOTS

Winning Spots	$1.00 Ticket Pays	$3.00 Ticket Pays	$5.00 Ticket Pays	$1.40 Ticket Pays
3	1.00	3.00	5.00	2.40
4	14.00	42.00	70.00	30.00
5	720.00	2,160.00	3,600.00	680.00

MARK 6 SPOTS

Winning Spots	$1.00 Ticket Pays	$3.00 Ticket Pays	$5.00 Ticket Pays	$1.40 Ticket Pays
3	1.00	3.00	5.00	1.20
4	4.00	12.00	20.00	6.60
5	88.00	264.00	440.00	120.00
6	1,480.00	4,440.00	7,400.00	2,200.00

MARK 7 SPOTS

Winning Spots	$1.00 Ticket Pays	$3.00 Ticket Pays	$5.00 Ticket Pays	$1.40 Ticket Pays
3				60
4	1.00	3.00	5.00	2.40
5	20.00	60.00	100.00	30.00
6	380.00	1,140.00	1,900.00	460.00
7	8,000.00	24,000.00	40,000.00	7,000.00

MARK 8 SPOTS

Winning Spots	$1.00 Ticket Pays	$3.00 Ticket Pays	$5.00 Ticket Pays	$1.40 Ticket Pays
5	9.00	27.00	45.00	12.00
6	80.00	240.00	400.00	120.00
7	1,480.00	4,440.00	7,400.00	2,300.00
8	25,000.00	50,000.00	50,000.00	25,000.00

MARK 9 SPOTS

Winning Spots	$1.00 Ticket Pays	$3.00 Ticket Pays	$5.00 Ticket Pays	$1.40 Ticket Pays
4				80
5	4.00	12.00	20.00	4.60
6	44.00	132.00	220.00	60.00
7	300.00	900.00	1,500.00	400.00
8	4,000.00	12,000.00	20,000.00	5,600.00
9	25,000.00	50,000.00	50,000.00	25,000.00

MARK 10 SPOTS

Winning Spots	$1.00 Ticket Pays	$3.00 Ticket Pays	$5.00 Ticket Pays	$1.40 Ticket Pays
5				280
6	20.00	60.00	100.00	28.00
7	136.00	408.00	680.00	196.00
8	960.00	2,880.00	4,800.00	1,400.00
9	4,000.00	12,000.00	20,000.00	5,320.00
10	25,000.00	50,000.00	50,000.00	25,000.00

MARK 11 SPOTS

Winning Spots	$1.00 Ticket Pays	$3.00 Ticket Pays	$5.00 Ticket Pays	$1.40 Ticket Pays
5	1.00	3.00	5.00	1.20
6	8.00	24.00	40.00	12.00
7	72.00	216.00	360.00	100.00
8	360.00	1,080.00	1,800.00	500.00
9	1,800.00	5,400.00	9,000.00	2,400.00
10	12,000.00	36,000.00	60,000.00	15,000.00
11	28,000.00	50,000.00	50,000.00	40,000.00

MARK 12 SPOTS

Winning Spots	$1.00 Ticket Pays	$3.00 Ticket Pays	$5.00 Ticket Pays	$1.40 Ticket Pays
5				1.20
6	5.00	15.00	25.00	6.00
7	32.00	96.00	160.00	40.00
8	240.00	720.00	1,200.00	300.00
9	600.00	1,800.00	3,000.00	800.00
10	1,480.00	4,440.00	7,400.00	2,000.00
11	12,000.00	36,000.00	50,000.00	10,000.00
12	36,000.00	50,000.00	50,000.00	50,000.00

MARK 13 SPOTS

Winning Spots	$1.00 Ticket Pays	$3.00 Ticket Pays	$5.00 Ticket Pays	$1.40 Ticket Pays
6	1.00	3.00	5.00	2.40
7	16.00	48.00	80.00	24.00
8	80.00	240.00	400.00	100.00
9	720.00	2,160.00	3,800.00	950.00
10	4,000.00	12,000.00	20,000.00	5,000.00
11	8,000.00	24,000.00	40,000.00	9,000.00
12	25,000.00	50,000.00	50,000.00	20,000.00
13	36,000.00	50,000.00	50,000.00	50,000.00

MARK 14 SPOTS

Winning Spots	$1.00 Ticket Pays	$3.00 Ticket Pays	$5.00 Ticket Pays	$1.40 Ticket Pays
7	1.00	3.00	5.00	4.40
8	10.00	30.00	50.00	11.00
9	40.00	120.00	200.00	44.00
10	320.00	960.00	1,600.00	350.00
11	1,000.00	3,000.00	5,000.00	1,000.00
12	3,200.00	9,600.00	16,000.00	4,000.00
13	16,000.00	48,000.00	50,000.00	15,000.00
14	25,000.00	50,000.00	50,000.00	30,000.00
	40,000.00	50,000.00	50,000.00	50,000.00

MARK 15 SPOTS

Winning Spots	$1.00 Ticket Pays	$3.00 Ticket Pays	$5.00 Ticket Pays	$1.40 Ticket Pays
6				2.50
7	8.00	24.00	40.00	10.00
8	28.00	84.00	140.00	32.00
9	132.00	396.00	660.00	150.00
10	300.00	900.00	1,500.00	400.00
11	2,600.00	7,800.00	13,000.00	3,000.00
12	8,000.00	24,000.00	40,000.00	13,500.00
13	25,000.00	50,000.00	50,000.00	30,000.00
14	32,000.00	50,000.00	50,000.00	40,000.00
15	40,000.00	50,000.00	50,000.00	50,000.00

Keno runners are available for your convenience. Since they must transport your tickets to the main counter for validation, please have the tickets ready as early as possible. We cannot accept responsibility if tickets are too late for the current game.

In most downtown Las Vegas casinos, the minimum bet is 70¢. For a 70¢ bet, divide the payoff by two.

That's the procedure for playing keno. You mark your ticket by putting Xs in crayon on the numbers you select, write the price of the ticket and total number of spots selected, and bring the ticket to the keno writer.

If you want to use a keno runner, you give her the money necessary to play the ticket you've marked, and she'll give you back a duplicate ticket. If there's a payoff, you can give her the winning ticket. She'll collect your winnings for you.

Remember—and this is very important—if you have a winning ticket, be sure to collect your winnings before the next game is called, or you'll forfeit the payoff.

In order to verify whether you won any money for a particular game, the keno writer will place a **punch-out** ticket over your ticket to see how many numbers have caught. A punch-out ticket contains, as the name implies, punch-outs of the numbers called. At the same time that the operator calls each number selected, that number is punched out automatically.

If in doubt about whether you've won, you can request the punch-out ticket and place your ticket under it.

Replaying the Ticket

Many players have favorite numbers they bet on, excluding all other numbers. They may select one group of numbers and keep playing them all day long. If you're that kind of player, you don't need to keep writing new tickets.

When you wish to replay a ticket, you simply hand in the duplicate ticket you've been issued by the keno writer. It now becomes the original, and you're given a new duplicate. You can exchange in this way indefinitely, until you get tired of the numbers, or until you finally hit it big.

How to Play Keno–Summary

1. Take a keno blank, whether in the keno lounge or in any area of the casino where keno runners are available, and X out the numbers you wish to play with the crayon that the casino offers.

2. After you've Xed out the numbers, add them up. There must be at least one and no more than fifteem numbers selected. Place this number of spots selected in the right hand margin of the ticket.

3. Choose the amount you want to bet, checking the rate card first to see the possible payoffs. After you've decided this, put that price without using either a dollar sign ($) or a cents sign (¢) in the box in the upper right hand corner of the blank ticket.

4. Take the ticket up to the keno writer or give it to a keno runner, after you pay the money necessary to play the ticket.

5. Verify that your ticket is marked correctly. When there's a dispute, the original ticket, the one you marked, predominates.

6. Watch the board to see if you've caught enough numbers for a payoff. If you have, then go up immediately, before the next game is called, and collect your payoff.

If you use a keno runner, have her collect for you by giving her the ticket and telling her there's money to be collected. She'll do it for you. It is customary to toke the runner in this event or the keno writer if you've collected a substantial amount.

7. If in doubt about winning, either check the punch-out ticket, or have the keno writer do it for you. He'll be happy to accommodate you.

8. You're not limited to playing one ticket. You can play several if you want, at one time, as long as you follow the procedure of marking them correctly.

9. You can replay your ticket, by either giving the duplicate to the keno writer, or handing it to the keno runner and stating that you wish to replay the ticket.

10. Don't fold or mutilate your ticket or mark it in any way. It's a very valuable commodity if you catch some winning numbers.

Straight Tickets

In the discussion concerning the writing of keno tickets, I showed how a straight ticket should be written and bet on. A straight ticket is the most common kind of ticket and can be marked with one to fifteen different numbers. The minimum amount it can be played for is usually 70¢ in downtown Las Vegas, Reno and Lake Tahoe, and $1 or $2 in the fancier hotels on the Strip.

Straight tickets can also be played for multiples of the minimum. Even if you're aiming to win $50,000, you don't have to bet too much over the minimum. For example, if you're playing a 12-spot (twelve numbers), a $1.40 bet entitles you to $50,000 if you hit all the numbers. When playing 13, 14 and 15 spot tickets, the same bet will get you $50,000.

With an 8, 9, 10 or 11 spot, however, you'd have to bet $3.50 to win $50,000, and the amount necessary to bet increases dramatically when playing smaller spot tickets. If you play a 6-spot, for example, it would take about

$32.20 (with all the numbers caught, of course) to win the $50,000.

Most beginning players, and even many experienced players, prefer the straight tickets. They're easy to play, and the payoffs are simple to calculate. These aren't the only tickets that can be written, though, and some others offer a variety of payoffs and possibilities, making keno even more interesting to play.

Split Tickets

A **split ticket** allows a player to write two or more tickets in one, splitting the numbers by either circling them or drawing a line between them. When writing a split ticket, the player is limited in that the numbers in one group can't be duplicated in the other group. They must be kept separate. A player may, however, mark one to fifteen numbers in each group. In the charts we'll look at in a moment, you'll see two split tickets, one separated by circling one group, and the other by drawing a line.

Before we examine these tickets, it's worth noting that you're not limited to two games at one time. If you want to, you can split the ticket three or more ways, as long as there are sufficient distinct numbers. For example, if you played 2-spots, you could split the ticket forty ways, but this kind of splitting isn't recommended.

One further note: some casinos will allow a player to bet on split tickets at a reduced rate, usually half of the minimum. Thus, if a player split a ticket into four tickets, where the minimum was $1, he could play for $2, each split ticket worth 50¢. If he catches enough numbers to win, though, the payoff will be one-half of what the rate card shows for $1.

Split Ticket—Circled Numbers

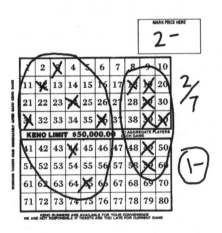

The above split ticket is made up of two 7-spots, each played for $1. The player should mark the total price in the upper right hand box, then mark 2/7 to show that two separate seven-spot straight tickets are being played as a split ticket. Next he should circle at the bottom margin the price for each individual split ticket.

To be doubly safe, inform the keno writer that this is a split ticket. The next split ticket is of 4-spots, the two parts separated by a line.

Split Ticket—Line Separated

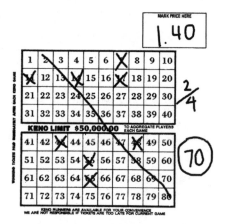

When playing a split ticket, you must remember that each split part is played as a separate ticket. So if you play two 6-spots and need to catch three numbers for a payoff, you'll have to catch all three on one of the split parts. You can't take two numbers from one part and one from the other for a payoff.

For split tickets, you don't have to have equal groups of numbers. You might split the ticket so that you're playing two 5-spots, one 8-spot, and three 2-spots, for example. On the margin of that ticket you'd write 1/8, 2/5, and 3/2, showing that you're playing one 8-spot, two 5-spots, and three 2-spots. You can play them for different amounts of money, but if you're playing at least two with the same spot total, you must play them for the same amount.

For example, you could play an 8-spot for $1, a 5-spot for $2, and a 2-spot for 70¢ each. If you add those up, you can see that you'd have to lay out $7.10 to play the ticket that way.

When you play split tickets, all groupings of the same number of spots must be for the same amount. In the above example, if you play one of the 5-spots for $2, the other 5-spot will have to be played for $2 also.

Way Tickets

A **way ticket** gives the player more versatility than a split ticket. A way ticket must have at least three groups of equal amounts of numbers. These equal groups combine with other equal groups to form several straight ticket combinations.

Unlike in the split ticket, here if you catch three numbers from one group and two from another, you have a winner. Here you combine, rather than separate, the individual groups. Way tickets can sometimes lead to big payoffs, because it's possible to win more than one way.

Let's examine a simple way ticket to see how such a win is accomplished. This ticket will contain three 4-spots, but it will not be written as a three 4-spot ticket, like a split ticket would. Instead it will be written as a three 8-spot, because with a way ticket we combine, rather than separate, the three groups.

The ticket would show three separate equal groups which combine to form three 8-spots. Here's how it's done: if we assume that group A consists of 13, 14, 23, and 24; group B consists of 42, 52, 53, and 63; and group C consists of 28, 37, 46, and 47, the three possible combinations are AB, AC, and BC. Thus, from three 4-spots, we can make three 8-spots. Next we must play them all at the same rate. On the Strip, there'd be a minimum of $1 per way, so our ticket would be for $3.

With an 8-spot, you must hit or catch at least five numbers to get a payoff. Since this kind of ticket is a little more complicated, I suggest you give the ticket to the keno writer after the game is called, just in case you've won something and are in doubt about it.

Combination Tickets

A **combination ticket** is a bit more complicated and much more versatile than either a split or way ticket. It gives a player many chances to win while playing just one ticket. You can create a ticket with three equal groups of 4-spots, setting up a combination ticket with three 8-spots and one 12-spot. The 12-spot is made by combining the three 4-spots. Each way is played for $1, so the ticket costs a total of $4.

We can go even farther with this same ticket and extend the ticket so that we are playing three 4-spots, three 8-spots, and one 12-spot, each for a dollar for a total of $7. There are many ways to win with this ticket.

Often combination tickets aren't played with equal groupings. The following is a good example of a versatile combination ticket containing three unequal groups of numbers.

Some casinos allow you to play at cheaper prices per way. Speak to the keno writer before playing any kinds of tickets but straight tickets, and find out the cheapest rates allowed.

As you can see, it can become quite expensive to play a game of keno if you're playing a number of ways at once.

If you write a very complicated combination ticket, go over it carefully with the keno writer and be sure it's written correctly. Because it may be difficult to determine if any payoff is required, also check with the writer after the game is called.

King Ticket

A **King ticket** is defined as any ticket in which there appears a single circled number. This single number is the **King**, which is never played alone. Instead, it's combined with other numbers to form various ways.

King tickets may have more than one King, and there are many King tickets that can be written. Because of their complex nature, King tickets should be carefully studied when used. Always consult a keno writer when you're not sure how to write the ticket or in doubt about whether you should receive a payoff. The writers will be happy to help, especially if you toke (tip) them for their aid.

Special Tickets

Some casinos will have **special tickets**,

with different rate structures. They vary from casino to casino, and they may also occasionally be changed.

When you're writing a special ticket, the casinos require that you mark it "sp" (for "special"), to differentiate it from the normal ticket paid according to the casino rate book.

Casino Advantage in Keno

The calculations to be made in keno are rather complex, and the permutations and combinations run into the millions. The advantage, however, is never less than 25% and runs up to about 35%.

The odds are strongly against the player, which is to be expected when the payoff is so great and the risk so small.

No matter what the special ticket is, and no matter what exotic payoffs the casino offers, expect to face these odds when playing keno.

Taxes on Keno Winnings

All gambling wins are taxable, and losses from gambling may be deducted from gambling winnings. The I.R.S. requires the casino to have a winner of $1,500 or more in a calendar year identify himself or herself by showing a driver's license, credit card, or social security card. The person's winnings will then be reported to the I.R.S., and the winner should report those winnings on his or her income tax return.

Nothing will be deducted from the winning amount unless the winner is a non-resident alien. In that case, 30% will be withheld from the winning amount and sent by the casino directly to the I.R.S. A Canadian citizen will have 15% taken out of his or her winnings.

When playing keno, have some identification with you so that, in case you do win a large amount, you can easily collect by showing the proper verifiable information and identification.

Playing Strategy for Keno

This game should not be played seriously for big money. There are many other games the casino offers with better odds for the player. If you are planning to play keno, then in order to take advantage of the game and to have a chance to win big money, I suggest that a player use the strategies below.

Avoid all games under 7-spots. With a $1 bet, you can win $18,000 in an 8-spot game,

WINNING KENO

$20,000 in a 9-spot game, and $25,000 in a 10-spot game. Check on the casinos; some pay more than others. In some casinos, a $1 bet on a 14-spot game will pay $25,000 if you catch all the numbers. In other casinos, the same bet and the same results might pay $40,000.

Playing for $1.40, you'll get $50,000 if you catch all the numbers on any 12, 13, 14, or 15-spot game in downtown Las Vegas.

If you want to play keno, it's better to risk $1.40 downtown than $2 on the Strip for the same payoff. Go to the keno lounge and check the rate cards in the casinos you enter. Look at them carefully. Shop around; don't throw away money. A 60¢ savings on each ticket adds up, because the game moves along quickly and rounds accumulate.

If you have favorite numbers, it's best to stick to them. There's nothing worse than going off a set of numbers only to watch them catch the next game without a payoff for you. Don't be oblivious to the numbers that come up frequently either. There may be a bias in either the ping-pong balls or the way they're blown around.

Some players pick numbers that haven't come up for a long time; others pick those that catch frequently. Keno is a game of chance. You take your chances when you pick num-

bers, since they'll be coming up in a random sequence.

Go for the big money no matter which numbers you want to play. The real enjoyment of keno lies in the possibility of winning that $50,000. Good luck.

Glossary of Keno Terms

Blank, Blank Ticket—A ticket marked with from 1-80 numbers not yet filled in by the player.

Board, Keno Board—An electrical setup showing the eighty numbers of keno in various parts of the casino, with the twenty selected numbers lit up as they are called.

Bowl—The cage that holds the marked ping-pong balls used in keno.

Caller—The casino employee who operates the blower and calls out the numbers selected.

Catch—A number selected by the player, which has been called by the operator of the game.

Combination Ticket—A ticket that allows groups of numbers to be combined with other groups.

Conditioning—The way a player decides to play his ticket written as fractions, such as 2/8 meaning two 8-spots.

WINNING KENO

Draw—Selecting a numbered ball into the goose at random.

Duplicate Ticket—The ticket marked in India ink by the keno writer and returned to the player.

Goose—Each of two transparent tubes holding ten balls apiece after they've been forced in by a hot air blower.

Group—Several numbers separated by other numbers through the use of a circle or line.

Keno Lounge—The area in which the game of keno is played, called and operated.

Keno Runner—A casino employee who collects players' tickets and bets, brings them to the keno writer, and, if there is a winning ticket, collects payoffs for the players.

Keno Writer—The casino employee who collects the player's bet, writes the duplicate, and pays off the winners.

King, King Number—A single separate number that combines with other groups of numbers to make a versatile ticket.

Original Ticket—The ticket filled out by the player and presented to the keno writer.

Punch-Out—The ticket belonging to the casino on which the selected twenty numbers for any game are punched out. Also known as a **draw ticket**.

Rate Card—The booklet issued by a casino

showing bets and payoffs on various spots selected by the player.

Special Tickets—Tickets other than the normal ones in the casino rate book, with special prices and payoffs.

Split Ticket—A ticket with two or more groups of numbers played separately.

Spot, Spots—These indicate the number of choices the player selects on a ticket. If the player selects five spots, it's a 5-spot ticket.

Straight Ticket—A ticket in which one to fifteen numbers are selected without combinations of any kind.

Way Ticket—A ticket with at least three different groups of numbers combining in various ways.

Writer—See **Keno Writer**.

Winning Slots

Introduction

This chapter will show you all you need to know to win money at slots. You'll learn which casinos to play in, what machines to play, and how to leave a winner. In recent years, new kinds of slot machines have been introduced into casinos throughout America. I'll familiarize you with the latest ones and show you how you can play for big money, into the millions of dollars in some cases.

That's not all you'll learn. There's a history of the slot machine and the various machines used in casinos and other locales over the years. There's inside information on how casinos set their slots, how the odds are figured and how to find jackpots that can make you rich.

By the time you finish this chapter, you'll be informed, entertained, and best of all, you'll be a winner at the slot machines!

History of Slots

The invention of the slot machine is credited to a Bavarian immigrant, Charles Fey, who, while working as a mechanic in San Francisco at the end of the 19th century, perfected a gambling device that was similar to the slots we're familiar with today.

The machines invented by Fey began to appear in bars and saloons around the Bay Area in the 1890s, and the payoffs were supposedly in free drinks if the correct symbols were lined up. One can only drink so much, though, and, as the players grew a bit more sophisticated, they demanded and got payoffs in coins.

There were ten symbols on each reel in these first machines, which were known as Liberty Bells. The symbols included the four playing card suits: diamonds, hearts, clubs and spades along with bells, horseshoes and stars. Since there were three reels, there were 1000 possible combinations that could be spun.

Of the early symbols used, only the bell remains as a symbol on modern slots. With the early slot machines, the payoffs were rather small by today's standards; a nickel for lining up two horseshoes, and the big payout, of ten nickels, for lining up three bells.

In those days, nickels as payoffs were a

big inducement to play the slots. A nickel could buy a beer or food at the bar and several nickels went a long way. The machines were rather small, able to fit on bar tops, where they were played by the saloon's customers. They became popular immediately, for people have always loved to gamble, and in a bar atmosphere, with alcohol loosening inhibitions, it didn't take much to get the patrons gambling.

The original Liberty Bells were made of cast iron, and were manufactured by hand, one at a time. Fey was a man who liked to stay on top of things, and he ran all ends of the business, including the collection of commissions. He split the profits from the Liberty Bells with the owners of the bars 50-50. The machines, as set by Fey, were quite lucrative and returned only 86% of the coins placed in them, giving Fey and the saloon owner a 14% profit.

After a while, these machines made direct cash payouts. The Liberty Bell took its place in gambling history as the first three-reel slot machine to have automatic payouts in coins. Although there had been other types of coin-operated gambling machines in use prior to Fey's invention, they were usually based on other games, such as roulette and dice, and were rather bulky affairs. None ever achieved the enormous popularity of Fey's slot machines.

He had, indeed, invented something that was a terrific money-maker. Here was a machine that took coins, showed a profit, made automatic payoffs, and didn't even need an employee to watch over its operation.

Alas, in those days, gambling devices weren't given patents. A man named Herbert Stephen Mills, who had been in the business of manufacturing carnival games that featured coin operated devices, was intrigued by the possibilities inherent in these machines. It didn't take long for Mills to get his hands on a Liberty Bell. He then hired away Mat Larkin, who was Fey's foreman, and after much reworking and redesigning of the Fey Liberty Bell, he was in the slot machine business.

Mills didn't drive Fey out of business, however, for the original inventor of the Liberty Bell kept at his essentially one-man business all the way into the 1930s. The Liberty Bell Saloon and Restaurant on South Virginia Street in Reno, Nevada which is run by grandsons of Charles Fey, has quite a collection of early slots, including the original Liberty Bells.

Mills, however, was much more of an enterprising businessman than Fey had been. The first Mills slots were ready for sale in 1906, and within a few short years, they were being sold around the country. From his earliest machine, the Mills Liberty Bell, Mills quickly moved to design and make others. The most popular of these were the High Top and Golden Falls.

The High Top and Golden Falls were blessed with a gimmick that really made gamblers want to play them. The Mills machines took in nickels, just as the Fey Liberty Bell had, but while the Bell nickels disappeared into the machine, never to be seen again unless there was a payout, the Mills machines were designed so that there was a window through which the player could see all the nickels already lost to the machine.

There they were, all those lovely coins, just waiting to be paid out. It was a tremendous design feature and made the Mills machines extremely popular and successful.

In the old Liberty Bells, only one row of symbols was visible. Mills improved this feature as well. Now a player could see three rows of symbols. This made the game much more exciting to the players. Now, even if they lost on any particular spin, they could see how close they had come to winning. If only that symbol had dropped another notch on the third reel!

Mills also increased the number of symbols on each reel to twenty, giving slots the number that was to remain as the standard for many years. With three reels, each containing twenty symbols, the possible combinations were raised to 8,000 (20 x 20 x 20).

Another innovation credited to Mills was the use of symbols that have become standard on many slot machines used to this day. The fruit symbols—lemons, plums and cherries—and the bell and bar are symbols players still see on modern machines.

Another concept that still remains to this day is the jackpot, the grand prize. It's what all slots players want to win; today it can be in the hundreds of thousands of dollars, and in some cases in the millions of dollars, instead of a handful of nickels.

In the 1930s, an owner of a Mills machine was hauled into court for illegally operating a gambling device. The judge, when sentencing the man, referred to the slot machines as one-armed bandits, and that's a term that has stuck to this day.

In fact, to take advantage of that term's popularity, some slots manufacturers made machines in the 1930s and 1940s that were in the shape of gamblers, and the handle was designed as an arm, becoming a literal, instead of a figurative, *one-armed bandit*.

WINNING SLOTS

Neither Mills nor Fey had a monopoly on slot machines. The demand was too great and the profits too easily made for this kind of un-patentable gambling device to be kept in the hands of two men.

One of the chief competitors featured the Watling Rol-a-Top. It had an escalator window on top of the machines, showing the last eight coins inserted. It became extremely popular, not only among the players, but also among the operators. The people who owned these machines liked the idea of being able to see whether recent coins inserted into the machine were slugs or the real McCoy. In the days when a nickel could buy a lunch, and men bit into half-dollars to see if they were genuine, the use of slugs was quite prevalent.

The list of manufacturers grew over the years. Names like Snyder, Daval, Rock-Ola, Southern Doll, Keeney, Evans and the Caille Brothers were common ones seen on various slot machines.

The Caille Brothers introduced a strange machine known as the Caille Gum Vendor, which could be placed in areas where slot machines were illegal if they paid off in coins. This machine paid off in gum instead of money, but that was a subterfuge, allowing the machine to be used without police interference. Other machines supposedly paid off in cheap candy, but when there was such a pay-off, the operator of the machine exchanged coins for the candy.

Still other machines had, in addition to the usual handle, devices called skill buttons. These buttons were supposed to be pressed to regulate the movement of the reels, but it was all a sham, since the pressing of the buttons had no control over the machines.

Today's machines, electronically operated, controlled by computer chips, have up to five reels and many symbols. There are sound effects as well as visual effects when they're played. Manufacturers such as International Game Technology and WMS have designed the machines not only to give themselves and the casinos a profit, but also to entertain the user while he or she plays the slots. In essence, they're still the same old "one-armed bandits" as far as casinos are concerned, for they still provide a major source of their income.

The Changing Game of Slots

Many casinos depend upon slots for much of their profits, and over the years, the casino executives have tried various ways to increase their slots income. In the early days of the casinos, the 5¢ play, the nickel, was the standard used in practically all of the clubs.

This lasted all the way into the early 1970s, but even though the casino income was quite good from this 5¢ play, the men who ran these establishments could see that they'd get five times the income if a 25¢ coin was played, and twenty times the nickel's profit if the dollar could be the standard unit of slot machine play.

To entice the bigger unit play, the casinos arranged with Bally, then the leading manufacturer of slot machines, to lease their $1 machines and make them the feature attraction in the slots area. These machines were then put into use as carousels: a number of machines were arranged in an oval, with but one changeperson in the center of the oval, on an elevated perch, changing cash into dollar coins or tokens.

In order to further entice the players, the casinos lowered their profit margin on the carousels, reducing it to 5% or less. This was the first time the casinos actually stated their **edge**, or profit margin, on slots they operated. If the edge was 5%, the casinos would trumpet that the $1 machines were *95% in the player's favor*. This was a bit misleading.

What it really meant was that for every

$100 played on the machines, the players would receive back $95. A more truthful observation would be that the machines were 5% *in favor of the casino*.

But a 5% and an even lower edge, often down to 2.5%, in those casinos that wished to cater to slots players, made these machines quite attractive. As inflation moved on in the United States in the 1970s and ensuing decades, the nickel wasn't worth much, and bought less and less.

What was the point of winning ten nickels at an old-fashioned slot machine when 50¢ couldn't even buy a cup of coffee in most places?

The 25¢ machines had bigger payoffs, but not really huge jackpots. The big thrill was now reserved for the dollar slots. To finally upgrade these machines, to get more in them, the casinos changed from a one-coin format to multiple coins.

Some of the 25¢ machines now required five or six coins to get all the possible payouts. On the $1 machines, a player had to risk at least three $1 coins to be eligible for the big jackpot.

After all those years of upgrading, the slots players were now accustomed to betting with dollars instead of nickels. This was perfect for the casino owners when the computer chip came into its own.

Now machines could be jazzed up to take many coins to win all kinds of jackpots, some running into the millions of dollars. New symbols were added, music was added, sound effects became common and the once lowly slot machine, a side income for many casinos, became a big money-maker.

Casinos that featured table games such as craps and blackjack took away most of these tables and became veritable slot machine jungles. Slots took off. Million dollar payoffs were now possible. Payouts of several thousand dollars were common. It was possible to put in some coins and come away with $50,000 or $100,000 or more.

There was another big improvement for both the clubs and the players in recent years. In the old days, there were a number or changepersons available to give coins in change for bills, in order for players to use the machines. Coins had to be fed into the machines constantly. Credits could be played off, but the process of starting with coins slowed everything down.

With the more sophisticated computer chips, the players didn't have to bother with coins at all. They could simply slip a bill—

either a $1, $5, $10, $20 or $100—into a money groove and get the appropriate credits shown on the machine. Only when the player cashed out, was he or she given coins.

Now changepersons are becoming relics. They're not needed to change bills into coins, since the machines do that automatically. Change booths are used by players now to get bills for the coins they have taken from the machine.

Soon, if the trends keep up, players will no longer cash in their winnings and get coins. In quite a number of casinos, tickets are issued when a player leaves the game. These tickets can be taken to a change booth and exchanged for money, or the tickets can be used at another machine.

With these improvements, the casinos' overhead is greatly reduced. All that is necessary is a slot mechanic in case a machine needs some adjustment or repair, and a changebooth and a random changeperson on the floor. The computer chip has radically changed the face of slots.

We'll examine the new machines available to today's players. They are much more exciting to play than the old-fashioned ones, with bigger payoffs and gigantic jackpots.

Millions of dollars can be won at one time

by a lucky player. These kinds of winnings have opened up slots to a whole new generation of players, people who are interested in hitting the big score, not grinding out dollars in the table games.

Slot Machines and Slots Players

There are basically two types of slot machines. The first kind are called straight slots, because the payoffs are rigid. The amounts shown as possible payoffs on the upper part or screen of the machine are what you can win— nothing more and nothing less—depending on the way the symbols line up on the reels. These machines are usually played with several coins.

Most of these machines will pay off when the correct symbols line up on the center payline. Others will pay off on any or all of the three paylines. Still others can pay out credits or coins when any or all of nine paylines are hit, taking into consideration the diagonal paylines on the machine.

On practically all machines allowing more than one coin to be played out at once, the machine will pay off less for one coin than it will for two, and so forth. In many modern machines, as many as forty-five or ninety coins can be played at one time, and the payoffs increase according to the coins put in. With all machines, the maximum number of coins permitted must be played to be eligible for the jackpot.

With the progressive machines, the jackpot increases with each play that doesn't yield a jackpot. Some of these machines are tied up to a bank of similar machines in the casino. Others, with enormous jackpots, are tied up to the same type of machine throughout the entire state of Nevada. All this is possible because of the computer chip.

Some of these jackpots begin at amounts like $100,000 and work their way up into the millions of dollars. With the Megabuck™ slots, it isn't unusual to see payouts for jackpots running close to $20 million dollars.

In fact, the biggest Megabuck™ jackpot ever recorded was $35 million. Even though it may be paid off over twenty-five years, that's still a lot of money to receive for getting lucky at the slots.

The casino executives and the manufacturers of the machines love it when there's a huge jackpot. It brings them not only publicity, but also (in the case of the casinos) hordes of slots players. Like outlets that sell winning lottery tickets, certain casinos get a reputation for jackpots and the customers pour in.

If you do hit a jackpot, a casino executive and several employees will come over and verify that you've won. You'll have to fill out a W2-G form for the IRS, and show identification, preferably something with your social security number. If you don't have a social security card with you, proper identification, such as a valid driver's license with a photo will do.

Depending on the machine, you'll either be paid in full, or you'll receive one-twentieth of the jackpot (1/25 for Megabucks™). The other installments will be mailed to you one at a time on the anniversary of your jackpot win.

What type of people play the slots?

Practically everyone who gambles tries his or her luck at them. Slot machines are exciting for all players, particularly those who may not understand table games or are hoping for the one jackpot that will ease their financial burdens and put them on easy street. The slots are ideal for people who want some excitement without having to risk too much, people who have a few extra bucks in their pockets and want to try their luck, hoping that lightning will strike and they'll leave the casino as wealthy individuals. In Nevada, a state where the population centers are swelling, the "locals" are big players of the slots, and there are casinos that cater just to them, putting out on the floor the most popular slots for their benefit.

Practically everyone, sooner or later, likes to take a chance at the slots. I know a few professional poker players, proud of their skills, who never gamble at other table games. But with a potential million or 18 million jackpot staring them in the face, they'll cash a $20 or $100 bill and take a shot.

Who plays slots? We all do. That's why this guidebook was written, not only give to you the flavor, the history, and the inside story of slots, but to show you how to give the machines your best shot.

Modern Slot Machines

I had mentioned how the casino owners, in order to increase their profits, began to eliminate the 5¢ machines, opting instead for the 25¢ and dollar slots.

This was before the advent of the computer chip; now there has been almost a direct reversal of the casino owners' attitude. Five cent machines appeal to a lot of gamblers, and the executives have found a way to keep these machines while maintaining high profits.

What they've done is put in enticing jackpots that are paid only when a maximum number of coins are bet, even though the coins are merely nickels.

To accomplish this, many nickel machines have nine paylines—three horizontal lines as well as the diagonal lines. In order to hit the jackpot, ten coins must be bet on each line. This means that nine lines times ten coins equals ninety coins, or $4.50 per play. This is a far cry from the old days when three nickels were bet for a total wager of 15¢. Four dollars and fifty cents per play is serious money. It's more than one bets on a dollar machine when betting two or three dollars at one time. With this added amount of money, the casinos' profits remain strong.

In many casinos, one can still see the old-fashioned machines, the straight slots, with fixed payoffs dependant on how many coins are placed in the machine. These are usually $1 slots that take one or two coins, with the payline in the center. Two coins played give the player twice the payoff as one coin.

You can still play these machines in a casino like the Mirage in Las Vegas, but their popularity has decreased with the advent of the newer slots, which have fancy symbols, music and pizzazz.

A higher percentage of casino profit is reflected in the 5¢ machines, which get more and more play each year and become particularly popular during recessions and hard times. Below is a list of some of these machines. Note that every day new machines are manufactured and put into play, but basically, the same principles apply.

5¢ Machines

Following are some 5¢ machines you may find in the casinos. (Note that with the constantly changing landscape of slots, you may find these in higher denominations or even phased out for newer models.)

Life of Luxury™ Has nine lines and ten coins can be played per line, for a betting total of $4.50 per play. The jackpot pays off 60,000 credits, or $3,000.

Who Dunnit™ Has nine lines and ten coins per line with a jackpot of 50,000 credits or $2,500.

Swinging Green™ Pays 100,000 credits for its jackpot and has nine lines and takes ten coins per line. This jackpot is worth $5,000.

Sticks and Stones™ and Creatures from the

WINNING SLOTS

Black Lagoon™ are similar with payoffs on jackpots totaling 45,000 credits.

Top Banana™, Jackpot Party™ and **Reel Em In™** Take twenty-five coins per play to be eligible for a jackpot of 20,000 credits for the first machine and 12,500 for the other two.

Double Bucks™ Pays up to 3,000 coins. It has cards, diamonds, money bags and gold statues as its symbols.

$1,000,000 Pyramid™ Pays a million dollars as its jackpot if the pyramid is completed. It's called a "winner's circle" bonus. Nine lines with ten plays per line must be played for the jackpot. Tickets as well as bills can be used or collected on this machine in some casinos.

Black Rhino™ A 5¢ machine with animal and flower symbols. It pays off 5,000 coins as its jackpot.

Red, White and Blue™ Rather old-fashioned machine with a pull handle as well as a button reading "play three credits." Three 7s on the center payline wins a jackpot of $3,000.

State Fair™ Pays a jackpot of $5,000 with nine lines and ten plays per line.

My Rich Uncle™ Has 9 lines and 10 plays per line, with a jackpot of 50,000 coins.

Texas Tea™ Similar to the above machine, but with an annoying voice commentary asking you if you want to be a millionaire in Texas oil.

The Munsters™ pays off 25,000 coins as its jackpot.

Austin Powers™ has characters from the popular movie displayed on the machine. The jackpot pays 75,000 credits. Nine lines with ten coins per line must be played for the jackpot. In one casino only tickets rather than coins are issued for payouts.

This is just a sampling of 5¢ machines. Note that the machines have names that are catchy, or refer to amounts of money or are based on popular characters from television or the movies. Having these characters, the casino owners figure, gives players a comfort zone in playing the slots.

Before going on to other machines of various denominations, I should explain what a ticket means, because as time goes by, more and more payouts will be made by ticket rather than by a player tediously collecting his or her coins as they spill into the well of the machine.

Ticket Payouts

There are still many machines that pay off in coins, but more and more are being switched to ticket payouts. When a machine can pay off with a printed ticket, there is generally a designation on the machine to show this. In the Station Casinos of Las Vegas, the designation is "Easy Pay."

Similar labels are shown in other casinos throughout the United States such as "Easy Play." Many Indian casinos have adopted the ticket payouts as well. International Game Technology is one of the manufacturers of these tickets, which bear the generic name of "ticket in, ticket out."

Since the ticket payout is printed in a cash denomination rather than in credits, machines that pay this way will show just how much the player has to his or her account in cash, rather than in credits.

For example, a nickel machine without a ticket payout option may show 85 credits. With the ticket cashout, the same machine will show the gambler's money credit to be $4.25. If the player cashed out at this point, the ticket would be printed for this amount. The slots player can now take this ticket to the cashier and get $4.25, or he or she could play this ticket in another machine that accepted such cashout tickets.

Monopoly™ Slots

This slot machine is very popular because millions of people played the game of Monopoly™ when they were children.

As a casino slots game, its symbols and board are familiar and comfortable to gamblers. It is primarily a 5¢ game with nine lines and five plays per line, for a total bet of $2.25. The machine has a base with symbols representing the game, such as "Chance" cards, while facing the player is a screen, known as a "bonus screen," that changes according to which paylines are covered.

In one version, Uncle Moneybags, the quintessential capitalist, sits astride a clear dome filled with colorful Monopoly™ money. When the bonus card is triggered, there's a "Money Grab."

There is also a special bonus when three "Chance" cards line up on an active payline. This two-tiered game is quite entertaining and popular, and is manufactured by WMS Industries, which runs a distant second to IGT, which is the foremost manufacturer of slot machine games.

Another version of the bonus screen shows the Monopoly™ board, based on the streets in Atlantic City, New Jersey, so familiar to millions of players of the board game.

Bonus payouts increase as the properties become more expensive. For example, the payouts range from four times the total bet on Mediterranean Avenue to ten times for any railroad to fifty times for Pacific Avenue and up to 300 times for Boardwalk.

A player can win up to 100,000 coins if he or she hits the jackpot on a nickel machine that adds up to $5,000. The bonus screen, when activated, is not only profitable but also entertaining to the player.

Another interesting game developed by WMS is Hollywood Squares®. This is based on the popular TV show produced by Whoopi Goldberg. It is a nine line, five reel nickel machine. Players reach various bonus rounds. A player reaching the second bonus round is asked a question and must pick the celebrity they think will answer it correctly. This feature makes the game much more interactive than others, which don't really have this kind of player participation. The jackpot is 25,000 coins.

WMS prides itself on its use of digital sound, second bonus rounds and advanced graphics, while its game themes use popular songs and recognized trademarks.

25¢ and $1 Machines

The most popular of the slot machines can be found in various price formats. For example, it is possible to play the Wheel of Fortune®

as a nickel, quarter or dollar machine. The 5¢ version, however, is radically different from the other two, with five instead of three reels and a fixed jackpot.

Spin For Cash™ is a quarter machine with a fixed $2,500 jackpot. Three coins must be played for maximum payoff. There is one center payline.

Spin The Wheel™ is another quarter machine. When the "spin the wheel" logo or symbol hits on the third reel center line, the player hits the "spin the wheel" button. There is a bonus multiplier, which must come on a black number, and totals from 35 to 4,000 coins ($1,000). There is also a double or nothing feature, so that the player can gamble even after hitting payoffs.

Elvis® is another quarter game. The jackpot starts at $200,000 and is progressive. There are three reels, with one to three coins that can be bet. Three coins are necessary for the progressive jackpot. One center line is the payline, and there are bonuses such as 500 coins for getting "jailhouse rock."

Money Masquerade™ is a quarter machine on which two coins have to be bet to win the progressive jackpot which is close to $50,000. It pays off when three Money Masquerade™ symbols hit on center payline.

Sinatra® is a dollar machine that can be played with one or two coins. With one coin there is a 500 credit; with two coins, the progressive jackpot comes into play. The machines are back to back, with each machine showing a likeness of the legendary singer and a city that he is associated with, such as Las Vegas, New York and Los Angeles. The jackpot is always in the hundreds of thousands of dollars. Three Sinatra® symbols have to line up on the center payline for the jackpot to be won.

Wheel of Fortune® comes in a 25¢ or $1 format that pays a jackpot when three Wheel of Fortune® symbols line up on the center payline. The jackpot at times runs over one million dollars. This is one of the most popular of the slots, for when the jackpot closes in on that million dollars, on weekends and evening hours, the seats are filled and people wait patiently to get into the game.

A feature of this game is a "spin" symbol only on the last of the three reels. When a player lands on the center line, he can press a "spin" button. A chorus chants "Wheel of Fortune" when this happens, just as it does at the beginning of the popular show. Above the game, a bonus wheel spins, and the lever can land in a number of places, paying from 20 to

1,000 credits. Wheel of Fortune® in its 25¢ version, has a jackpot that starts at $200,000. The $1 machine starts at $1 million for its jackpot. The quarter version of the game is the most popular slots game ever manufactured by IGT. **Megabucks™** is another machine manufactured by IGT. It's tied up to all other Megabucks™ machines in a particular jurisdiction, such as Nevada, California, New Jersey or Mississippi. The progressive aspect of its jackpot payoff makes it the most exciting of all slots to play, because it has the biggest payout. The jackpot, when hit, is in the millions of dollars, ranging from $10 million to more than $35 million. When the three Megabuck™ symbols line up on the center line, and three coins have been bet, the winner is a multimillionaire.

To keep the machine exciting, IGT, the manufacturer, starts the progressive jackpot at $7 million in Nevada, $3 million in California at the Indian casinos, and $4 million in the casinos of Atlantic City. There are smaller payouts in the thousands of dollars, as, for example, when three "double diamond" symbols hit on the center line with a three coin play.

Summary

There are many other machines in all the categories we covered. The machines you've seen in this chapter are just a sampling of what one can play and win in a casino.

Most, like Megabucks™, pay out jackpots in twenty equal installments. Some, like the $1,000,000 Pyramid™, Elvis®, Addams Family™, Party Time™ and Visual Jeopardy® are paid off in their entirety when a player wins the jackpot.

IGT has an arrangement with the casinos so that its machines are leased or given to them for a share of the ongoing cut of the profits. Most machines are otherwise bought outright. The big money made by the casinos on slots is when they own the machines, and there has been an ongoing dispute between a number of casinos and IGT over this.

The Mathematics of Slots

The casinos, before the advent of the computer chip, were allowed to set the slot machines to give themselves whatever percentage of profit they desired. They didn't have to answer to anyone. The best part, as far as the casino owners were concerned, was that they didn't have to tell the customers, the people actually playing the machines, just what their percentage of profit was.

The owners can still manipulate their profits, particularly on the older machines, with fixed jackpots, a center payline, and a machine that takes from one to three coins, of whatever denominations.

On the newer machines, particularly those tied up to many casinos to increase the jackpots, the manufacturers have built-in profits which are tied to computer chips.

And the profits are enormous, even on the 5¢ machines, which now force the player to bet $2.25 or $4.50 per play to be eligible for the jackpot.

That's a big bet each time a player hits the button that starts the reels spinning. Many players can't afford to bet this amount, and when playing a 5¢ machine with nine lines and ten plays per line, often bet one coin per line or nine coins (45¢) rather than the $4.50 necessary to be eligible for the biggest payouts.

With the basic machines, there are three reels with each reel holding twenty symbols. Most of the symbols on these machines are familiar to players, such as cherries, 7s, bars and so forth. Let's take a look at such a machine.

The first thing we want to know is how

many possible combinations can be made from these three reels and twenty symbols. To do this, we multiply 20 x 20 x 20. Doing this, we come up with 8,000 possible combinations.

Now we know that the machine must be played 8,000 times to get the full cycle of combinations played out. The casino executives know this also, and they base their profit projections on these 8,000 spins. They have their mechanics set the payoffs so that a certain number of coins are retained, and these coins, divided by the 8,000 possible spins, determines their profit percentage.

For example, suppose the machine, after the full cycle is finished, retains 800 coins. Then the house win percentage would be 10%. More coins retained give a higher winning percentage to the house; fewer retained coins gives a lower percentage to the casino.

With these basic machines, the player will see a bigger casino percentage win at Strip hotels and casinos catering to high rollers. Those hotels, such as the big opulent ones on the Strip, look to table games as their primary source of gaming income, with the slots secondary. On the other hand, the Las Vegas downtown casinos and the smaller ones in Nevada cater for the most part to lower level gamblers and "locals," the people who live in town. Their slots will be *looser*, giving more money back to the players.

In those casinos catering to locals and the small players, other inducements will be offered by the casino in the way of money, prizes and goods. To further encourage players, practically every casino offers free membership cards, which are inserted into the machine when the player starts gambling, and keep track of the play by computer. The more the gambler plays, the more credits his cards build up; these credits are paid off through various perks, such as free meals, T-shirts and all kinds of prizes.

In the age of the computer, the huge jackpots are on machines manufactured by companies such as IGT and WMS, and these are electronically mastered by computer chips, with the casino having no control over the machines directly.

When a payoff is made, it's paid by the manufacturer, with the casino itself merely sharing in the profits the machines engender. Only when the slot machines are owned outright by the casinos can the slots mechanics manipulate the payoffs, but even this may become a thing of the past as everything is increasingly done through the computer chip.

With the chip, it's difficult to know exactly what the machine takes in and what the break-even point on the gigantic jackpots are. When IGT sets up a minimum jackpot of $7 million before even one play on its Megabucks™ machine, you can be sure that before anyone hits the jackpot, a lot of money will have been split between IGT and the casinos where the machine is installed.

There's also the twenty-five year splitting of the payout, which gives IGT even more profits, since it can buy an annuity to cover the payouts.

Winning at Slots

My mother had the best philosophy about winning at slots, but it's dull work and tends to lead to headaches and backaches. She'd walk around the casino looking into the wells of all the slots, the wells being the small metal device that holds coins falling from the machine after a win.

Occasionally she found a couple of nickels left over by a slots player. A few times she collected a bunch of quarters and once an Ike dollar. But even my mother succumbed to the lure of the slots and with a cousin played a quarter machine, each of them taking half of a $10 roll of quarters. After four or five spins, a

$50 payout came down, and my mother wanted to quit then and there.

The cousin felt that this was merely the prelude to the $1,000 jackpot that the machine offered, and kept putting in quarters. When the roll was exhausted, my mother insisted on splitting the $50 and took away half of the $40 gain, for a nice little profit. As I said, she wasn't much of a gambler. With her profits in her purse, she watched her cousin run through his share, then take out another $10 and lose that also.

"I always want to quit a winner," said my mother, and that's pretty good advice for anyone to follow.

There will be times when you're ahead on a particular machine. If you're substantially ahead, there's no more foolish feeling than giving back all the coins you've won on that same machine. Take some profits and leave. Get some coffee, or take a break of some kind. Then try another machine a little later on.

Which machines are best to play?

That's a question that often is asked, and we'll try and answer it as best we can. In the pre-computer chip days, when each casino pretty much owned their own machines and could set them for various percentage payouts, it was not so much which machines to play, but where to play them.

As I mentioned before, there were certain casinos that catered to slots players. The machines were looser there; in addition, slots players were entitled to free drinks and sometimes food. There were usually giveaways and prizes to be offered.

Today, however, practically all casinos offer membership cards which are inserted into a slot in the machine, and these cards track the time and money spent by each slots player. The casino offers benefits to those players, and no matter where you play slots these days, cocktail waitresses are available to give you any kind of drink you want, whether it's a soft drink or a scotch on the rocks.

Since the gigantic jackpot payoff machines are tied to a particular jurisdiction rather than a single casino, it doesn't really matter where you play these days, if you're attempting to win serious money in the hundreds of thousands or millions of dollars.

Whether you play a Wheel of Fortune™ quarter machine in a posh Strip hotel, a downtown "sawdust joint," or way out in the east or western sides of town in a casino that caters to locals, the payoffs will be the same. This is because the Wheel of Fortune™ quarter slots is tied in with every other machine of the same kind throughout Nevada.

In other words, you can just as well be playing in Wendover or Mesquite if they have those machines there. The chances of winning the jackpot are the same and so is the payout. A bit of common sense and awareness of the situation should also prevail. For example, a Wheel of Fortune™ quarter machine jackpot starts at $200,000 and works its way up from there. This is the most popular of all the Wheel of Fortune™ slots, and the jackpot quickly escalates. Compare that to the same dollar machine whose jackpot begins at $1 million.

Recently, when checking out these machines, I found that the quarter machine had a jackpot of $1.7 million, while the $1 slots was showing a $1.4 million jackpot.

Why bother playing the dollar machine for a lower jackpot when the quarter machine not only has a bigger jackpot, but has been played much longer without a jackpot?

To cap it all off, by playing the quarter machine, you're investing one-fourth as much money as you would in the dollar machine. Taking all these factors into consideration, you'd have to agree that it would be foolish not to try your luck at the quarter slots.

This is the intelligent way to play. First,

scout around for the kind of machine you feel comfortable with, and that suits your bankroll. Then also think of your goal.

Do you want to take a shot at a huge jackpot, or would you be satisfied with a machine that has a smaller jackpot but more frequent smaller payouts?

Machines with smaller jackpots do tend to give more frequent small payouts, because the manufacturers of these machines as well as the casino operators know that, when you're going for a jackpot over a million dollars, you're looking for the big payoff, and aren't that concerned with the smaller ones. The jackpot machines are structured to give less frequent payouts of smaller sums than the machines that have jackpots in the thousands of dollars.

I was recently speaking to an executive with IGT, who commented on the Wheel of Fortune™ jackpot winners. Invariably, she said, the players were excited by the bonus wheel that paid off up to one thousand credits and when they hit the big jackpot of over a million dollars, they were surprised.

Interviewing people in casinos playing the Wheel of Fortune™, I've found that they're most interested in that spin button being pressed and the wheel of fortune spinning.

They wait for the "Spin" symbol to land on the center line in the third reel and the chorus to shout "wheel of fortune," and then find out just what they've won, even though it's not a jackpot.

This "Spin" aspect of the machine is certainly what gives it tremendous popularity.

Another important aspect is how much money you'd be comfortable losing, whether it's emotionally or financially. Even the nickel machines can get very expensive, when you have to play forty-five or even ninety coins or credits at once for the maximum payout.

Players find that it's cheaper to put in $2 in $1 slots rather than ninety nickels, and go after a larger jackpot. You must be comfortable when playing; if the loss will devastate you, don't play.

I can't emphasize this enough. Only very few win the big jackpots compared to the millions who play the slots, and unless you get some big payouts, the money drains away. You must be prepared for this.

Winning at the machines is a matter of luck. No skill is involved in pressing a button to start the reels moving. They still move the same old way, one at a time, until the first reel is complete, then the second, and finally the third. You can verify this next time you're at a machine like Wheel of Fortune™.

What is important in playing these machines is to be comfortable. Don't go overboard, and never play with money you can't afford to lose.

In casinos where the house can fix the win percentages, the operators generally put loose machines along the outside, next to where lines form for shows or meals. Players waiting to be seated play these machines and are pleasantly surprised by the payouts, so, after they've eaten or seen the show, they linger in the casino to try their luck at other slots.

When the operators control the payouts, another thing they do is place a loose machine next to a tight one. What one player makes the other gives back.

Use common sense. If one jackpot is bigger than another, and all other factors are the same, go after the bigger jackpot. Studying this book will have given you some idea of where jackpots begin.

If you know that the quarter Wheel of Fortune™ jackpot starts at $200,000 and goes up above $2 million, why play it when it stands at $350,000, for example. Be patient. It's not going anywhere. You may have a limited time to gamble when you are on vacation, but you still must play intelligently. Look for the biggest jackpots, or for machines that pay off frequently and allow you to leave a winner.

Using and following these principles will give you a chance to end up a big winner. I looked up a list of jackpots hit during the month of January 2002 in Las Vegas. Someone won $1.2 million on an Addams Family™ nickel machine, and was paid instantly.

That same week a twenty-eight-year-old man won $1.9 million on a Wheel of Fortune™ quarter machine. He had invested a grand total of $30 before the big payoff. Finally, a Hawaiian visitor won $3.7 million on a quarter machine she had played for less than $20.

None of them invested very much money, before the jackpot hit. You could be the next big winner! Good luck.

Money Management

Whether you play slots for fun or as a serious endeavor, it's important to manage your money correctly. You want to be a winner in the long run, and to do this, you have to leave a winner.

Often, what happens is the following: a player will start to hit some good scores on a machine and find himself or herself ahead by a couple of hundred dollars. Then, stubbornly, the player keeps on feeding coins or credits into the machine, and ends up losing them all back, and leaving the seat a net loser. That's what you don't want to happen.

Protecting Your Wins

If you find yourself ahead, let's say $250 at a $1 machine, mentally put $200 aside and play out the $50. Let's assume that the machine takes three coins or credits at a time. Then you play $48 or $51 worth of coins. If you lose this amount, cash out and leave the seat.

You've netted a nice win, and have that money for a later play at another machine.

We're now discussing straight slots, where the jackpot is of a fixed limit. If you're winning, you must start thinking about leaving the seat as you feed more coins or credits into the machine, and you watch the coins you've already won melting away.

Remember this and remember it well: one of the fallacies of gambling is thinking you're now playing with the casino's money. It's not the casino's anymore; it's yours and you must protect it. Take a profit and leave.

Playing to Win

I keep emphasizing the word "winner," because it's an important word to a slots player. The whole purpose of playing the machines is to win. The casino wants a profit from its machines. So should you. If you have the profit, keep it.

Playing for the Megabuck Payoff

When you're playing a machine that has a progressive jackpot, one that is in either the hundreds of thousands of dollars or even higher, in the millions, there will be fewer smaller payouts to sustain you as you go after the big bucks.

What you want is the gigantic payout. You are investing so much money per hour to get at the big jackpot. It's a longshot, but this is an opportunity to become rich in one fell swoop, with a little luck.

The odds are against you, of course, for the chances of winning millions are calculated almost the way lotteries are calculated, as millions to one against the player. Someone will eventually win, and it may be you who gets lucky. If you're going after that gigantic payout, then you must expect to lose money while trying, just as you would in a multi-million dollar lottery.

WINNING SLOTS

The thing to do is play and plan sensibly and sanely. Set aside a reasonable amount of money to try for that jackpot. This should be money you can afford to lose, money that won't hurt you financially or emotionally. When you've used up the money, as may happen, stop playing. Use your head and control your emotions.

Even with the million dollar jackpots, you may be ahead of the game while playing. Recently I played a Wheel of Fortune™ quarter machine with a jackpot of $1.97 million. I slipped in a $20 bill and got eighty credits. I hit a few of the "Spin" logos and found myself ahead about 250 credits.

I was tempted to leave but I wanted to go after the big jackpot and my plan was this: when I got back down to eighty credits and broke even, I'd get up. Well, the machine went down to 83 credits, and I hit the button and got two triple diamond logos and a bar on the center line, and 720 credits piled up.

Now I had 803 credits or a little less than $201. I glanced at my watch. I had been playing close to an hour; it was late and I was tired. One more spin of the wheels brought me down to 800 credits. I cashed in the 800 and left with two bucketfuls of quarters and $200. I was satisfied–I had left a winner.

As noted, keep discussing control, sanity and limited wins. Follow this advice and you won't get hurt and you may even find yourself collecting a small fortune when that jackpot hits.

A Short Slots Story

As a writer in Las Vegas, I hear a lot of stories, good and bad. Poker players tell me stories of their "bad beats," hands that they should have won but were beaten with, and roulette players let me know how close they were to a gigantic payout, if only their lucky number had come up twice in a row.

Recently, I was sitting in a keno lounge in a Strip casino, just relaxing, when an elderly lady sat down next to me, and, after a few minutes, we got into a conversation. She was waiting for her son, she informed me, and had traveled from a small town in Michigan to meet him in Las Vegas two days before.

I told her I lived in Vegas, and she nodded thoughtfully. "It's very exciting," she said, and told me she was thinking of playing the slots, but was living basically on social security. She was intrigued by jackpots that would certainly change her lifestyle.

WINNING SLOTS

I told her not to gamble if she was un-
comfortable playing, but she said she had put
aside fifty dollars for that purpose and she
asked me what to play.

"I want to sit down while I play," she told
me, "I'm eighty-two."

"Do you know how to play games like
blackjack?"

"Oh, no, I was thinking of the slot machines. Which ones are best?"

"Well, with $50, I'd play one that took two
quarters at the most, and had a reasonable jackpot."

"That sounds like a good plan. Wish me
luck."

I wished her luck, and then her son came.
After introducing him to me, she said good-
bye and I watched her walk slowly with him.
She limped slightly and I thought a walker
would help her, or at least a cane. Some elderly ladies are too vain to use them, as my
mother had been till her last days.

The next night, walking through the same
casino, I heard a familiar voice. I turned and
saw the same lady, sitting in a chair by a slots
machine. She told me her son was playing
craps and she was waiting there for him, not
playing, just resting.

"How are you doing?" I asked.

"Oh, fine…fine. You gave me good advice."

"Did I?"

"I played one of those quarter machines, and don't you think I won."

"The jackpot?"

She nodded, a big grin on her face.

"How much did you win"

"Three thousand dollars. I couldn't believe it when it happened. You know, this is the first time I ever really won anything. In my entire life."

"That's wonderful. That should pay for your trip and then some."

"Yes it will. And do you know what I'm going to do with the money?"

I looked at this sweet woman, so relaxed and happy now.

"My great-granddaughter wants to go to a horse camp, to learn to ride, and now I can afford to send her. Isn't that wonderful?"

"It is indeed. God bless you," I said, touching her arm lightly. "You're a good woman." Thoughts of my own mother flooded into my memory.

"Well, you take care," I said, turning away. I walked through the casino with a lighter step, watching the shrieking gamblers at the tables, feeling good. Really good.

Glossary of Slots Terms

Big Bertha—A slang term for a type of huge machine that contains from eight to ten reels and an oversized handle. At one time it was kept near the front entrance of casinos as a lure to prospective gamblers.

Bonus Screens—In many of the modern slots, facing the player, this screen shows the extra payoffs that can be gotten if paylines are hit.

Carousels—An area that was set aside for a group of $1 machines, ringed in an oval around a changeperson.

Center Payline—The middle of three lines on a machine, which usually must be filled with symbols for a correct payout.

Change Area—The place where slots players can get change or be paid off from their coins or tickets. Usually, no chips can be redeemed here. They must go to the cashier's cage.

Changeperson—The casino employee who makes change for slots players. They usually roam around the slots area.

Credits—Instead of coins being paid off after each win, the number of coins credited to the player shows up as "credits."

Jackpot—The ultimate or highest payout on any slots machine.

Liberty Bell –The name given by the inventor Charles Fey of San Francisco to his original slot machine.

Lines—The number of possible payout lines, usually from three to nine.

Loose, Loose Machine—A slots machine that pays out often and gives the house just a small edge over the player.

Mechanic, Slots Mechanic—A casino employee who sets the slots machines for their payouts, and also repairs any machine needing work.

Megabucks™—As of this writing, these are the machines with the biggest jackpots, running up to $35 million.

Mega Jackpot™ Machines—These machines, manufactured by IGT, have huge jackpots that are paid off either at once or in some cases, over twenty years.

Mills Machines—These were the first machines used nationwide, and the first to use both standard symbols and a jackpot.

One-Armed Bandit—The popular term for the slot machines, going back to the days when the player had to pull a handle to get the reels moving.

Paylines—The horizontal lines on a machine, which pay off. Usually one center line is the payline, but up to nine are seen on many modern machines.

Plays—When seen on a machine, this category shows the number of coins or credits that can be played on any spin; "ten plays" means ten coins or credits.

Progressive Machines—Machines with no designated limit jackpot, whose jackpot instead increases each time a coin is inserted or a credit is used and no jackpot comes up.

Reels—The vertical rows on a slot machine. The standard is three, but as many as five or even more can be seen on certain machines. Each reel usually contains twenty symbols, but some slots contain even more.

Slots—Another term for the slots machines.

Straight Slots—Machines that have a designated fixed jackpot.

Symbols—The various representations such as fruits or bars on a slot machine reel. Many casinos put in their own logos for the big payouts, as do manufacturers.

Ticket—More and more frequently, a player will receive a printed ticket from a machine after a win, so that he doesn't have to wait for coins to fall in order to collect his payoff.

Tight Machine—A slots machine that pays out infrequently, thus giving the house a big advantage over the player.

Well—The bottom metal area of the machine

where payout coins fall to and are collected by the player.

Wheel of Fortune™—The most popular game in history, of those manufactured by IGT, the leading maker of slots machines.

Window—The area in front of the machine which shows the lineup of reels and symbols.

Winning Roulette

Introduction

Roulette is a game that has fascinated and intrigued millions of players over the years. It's not only a leisurely game, but an exciting game as well.

You'll be playing the same game that has attracted kings and queens, prime ministers and statesmen, millionaires and captains of industry.

Roulette has a great variety of bets available, more than in any other casino table game. Betting choices may be paid off anywhere from even money to 35-1, and bets can overlap, with the same numbers covered in several ways.

Because of this factor, the game has attracted systems to beat it from the first time it was introduced. We'll show you the more popular ones and the pitfalls involved.

You'll find out details about both the American and European game, including the possible wagers and payoffs involved, so that you'll be able to play this most fascinating of games intelligently.

American Roulette

The Dealer

In American casinos, the game is run by one dealer. This is in contrast to the European version of roulette, in which several **croupiers** (the French term for dealer) are used, since the European game is played with a double layout, and more employees are needed to staff the table.

In American casinos, one dealer will suffice to run the game. Sometimes, if the game is particularly busy, the dealer may have an assistant, whose sole function will be to collect losing chips and stack them. This is the exception, not the rule.

The dealer has several duties. He or she will first change the player's cash into roulette chips. Each player will receive roulette chips of a different color from the other players' chips. These roulette chips are specially marked and have no intrinsic value away from the roulette table. The different colors make for a smoother game, since there will usually be a multitude of bets on the layout, and the only way the dealer will know how to make proper payoffs will be through the color of the chips.

In addition to changing cash for chips, the dealer runs the game. He keeps the wheel spinning, and he rolls a small white ball in the opposite direction, letting it spin until it falls into a slot on the wheel. This slot determines the winning number and other payoffs.

After a winning number is determined, the dealer collects all the losing chips first, then pays off the winning bets. The players then make new bets on the next spin of the ball, and the whole procedure is repeated.

There is usually a pitboss in the vicinity of the roulette wheel. He or she may supervise the play at the table and will be called upon if there is a dispute between the players and the dealer or between two or more players. Disputes rarely happen, though, since all players use different colored roulette chips.

Roulette Chips

As I mentioned, the chips are different colors than other casino chips and are marked differently. A player can't wager them at any other game in the casino. Players are also forbidden from taking these chips away from the roulette table. When they've finished playing, they must return all their chips to the dealer, who will pay off the player by exchanging these for casino chips, which can then be brought to the cashier's cage and exchanged for cash.

There is usually a standard value placed on the roulette chips. In the old days, before inflation, 10¢ or 25¢ chips were the standard. Today, it's hard to find a standard chip value less than $1. If a player gives the dealer a $20 bill, he or she will receive twenty chips, each with a value of $1.

The values of chips are not fixed, however. Suppose that a player came to the roulette table with a $100 bill and wanted each chip to be valued at $5. The player will request this valuation of the dealer, and the dealer, to be certain that no mistakes will be made later, will place a chip of the player's designated color on the outside rim of the wheel with a $5 marker on it, or a button to show that a stack of twenty chips is worth $100.

Where no chips are on the rim, everyone is playing with the standard value chips. These chips will come in enough colors, usually eight or ten different ones, to accommodate that many players. There will also be enough chairs at the roulette table for that number of players.

Players may change the valuation of their chips during the game. If a player won a lot of money, rather than continuing to bet with $1 chips and using handfuls of them, he could change the valuation of his chips to $5 each. He would simply have to turn them in to get them re-valued, or he might be given chips of a different color.

For bigger bets, such as $5, $25, or $100, the casino allows a player to use standard casino chips. Although players occasionally bet with standard casino chips or cash, this practice is not recommended since it can cause confusion about who owns those chips or that money. The vast majority of bets will be made with roulette chips.

When payoffs are made, the dealer *cuts* the chips, or breaks them into stacks. If the payoff is seventeen chips, for example, he'll cut a stack of twenty by taking three chips off the top. He'll then move the rest of the stack to the winner.

In contrast, in a European game, a **rake** is used to collect and pay out chips. In both games, after the number has come up, some kind of marker is placed on the layout to indicate the winning number before the losing chips are collected and the winning bets are paid off.

The American Wheel

The game of roulette depends on the spin of the wheel, an ornate device (see diagram below) that is approximately three feet in diameter and contains slots numbered from 1 to 36, plus a 0 and 00.

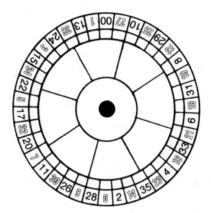

The bowl of the wheel, which takes up most of the wheel's space, contains numbered pockets. Above this bowl are eight metal buffers, some horizontal and some vertical, which are there to slow the ball as it spins counter to the wheel's motion, so that it will fall into a pocket in the most random manner possible.

When the ball falls into a pocket, that pocket corresponds to a particular number. The number determines which bets win and which lose for that spin of the wheel.

Each pocket is separated from its neighbors by metal dividers, known as **separators**. As the ball slows, it may fall into a pocket only to bounce up and into another pocket. Eventually inertia will cause it to remain in one pocket, and the number on that pocket wins for that spin.

There are thirty-six numbers in all, half in black and half in red, plus two extra numbers, the 0 and 00, which are in green. The numbers are not in consecutive order on the wheel. Rather, they are placed randomly, with red and black numbers alternating, except when interrupted by the 0 and 00.

With thirty-six numbers on the wheel, half are odd while half are even, half are black while half are red, and half are in the lower tier (1-18) while half are in the higher tier (19-36). All of these categories are possible bets: odd or even, red or black, high or low. As we shall later see, they are paid off at even money.

If there were only thirty-six numbers, the house would have no advantage over the player. Roulette would merely be a game of chance, without either side, the bettor or the casino, having an edge. The addition of the 0 and 00, however, gives the house a definite advantage of 5.26%. These could be called **house numbers**, because they are winning numbers for the house when the player bets on any of the even money propositions just mentioned, as well as when the player bets on other numbers and possibilities.

A gambler can bet on the 0 or 00 as numbers, just as he bets on any other numbers. In that case, though, there are thirty-eight possible numbers to bet on, with the payoff at 35-1 for a single number. The casino still has a 5.26% advantage.

Because the house has a built-in advantage, it wants the game to be played as honestly as possible. The roulette wheels, therefore, are built to be as friction-free as possible, so that there is no *bias* or deviation from a random situation prevailing. The wheels are inspected frequently and checked for any worn parts, such as pockets or dividers, since a worn part may create a bias.

Some players go from wheel to wheel, clocking them and checking out the pattern of numbers that come up, hoping for a bias. They rarely find one. If numbers seem to come up in any sequence out of the ordinary, it's probably coincidence. Even when there's a random sampling, numbers can repeat and appear to be in a strange sequence. Believe that the spins are still the result of chance.

The Roulette Layout

Now we come to the partner of the wheel at the roulette table: the layout. The layout contains all the possible betting situations that a player can use in roulette. The following is a typical roulette layout.

		0		00
		1	2	3
1 to 18	1st 12	4	5	6
		7	8	9
EVEN		10	11	12
		13	14	15
◇	2nd 12	16	17	18
		19	20	21
◆		22	23	24
		25	26	27
ODD	3rd 12	28	29	30
		31	32	33
19 to 36		34	35	36
		2-1	2-1	2-1

The layouts are usually green. The numbers from 1 through 36 are divided into three columns and are in numerical order. Each one is either red or black, corresponding to the colors on the wheel. 0 and 00 are at the head of the columns of numbers, and players may bet on them separately or together.

On the outside are the **even money bets**: 1-18, even, red, black, odd, and 19-36. Between them and the columns are the **dozens bets**: 1-12, 13-24, and 25-36, placed so that they correspond with the numbers in the columns. On the layout these dozens bets are marked, "1st 12," "2nd 12," and "3rd 12."

Finally we have the **columns bets**, which are at the far end of the columns, opposite the 0 and 00 areas. They each show 2-1, the price at which they are paid off. Each of these column areas covers all the numbers running down that column.

This layout is standard in American casinos. As we have said, it will accommodate all the possible bets that can be made at the roulette table.

Inside Bets

Because they take place within the thirty-six numbers, 0 and 00, the bets we'll be discussing in this section are called **inside** bets.

With the exception of one bet, the Five-Number bet, which gives the house a 7.89% advantage, all the following wagers in American roulette give the house an edge of 5.26%.

Let's begin with a favorite of roulette players the world over.

Straight-Up Bets

Single number bet; pays 35-1.

When a chip is placed on a single number, as shown on the layout below, this wager is called a **straight-up bet**. If the number comes up, the payoff is 35-1. If any other number comes up, including 0 or 00, the bet is lost.

A single number bet can be made on any number on the layout, including all numbers 1-36, as well as 0 and 00. No matter which number the player selects, the payoff will always be 35-1.

A player is not limited to one straight-up bet. He may make as many as he desires, and place as many chips on a single number (up to the house limit) as he wishes. For example, a player can put five chips on number 0, two on number 4, and one each on numbers 12, 15,

23, and 34. No one will object, and since your chips will be a distinct color, they won't be confused with anyone else's.

To bet correctly, place your chip in the center of the numbered box, making sure not to touch any of the surrounding lines. If you touch the lines, you might have another kind of bet.

If another bettor likes your number and has placed a chip in that box, his wager doesn't preclude your making the same one. Simply place your chip (or chips) on top of the other player's. This is a perfectly valid way to bet. The house edge on such a bet is 5.26%.

Split Bets

Two numbers bet; pays 17-1.

In order to make a **split bet**, you should place your chip or chips on the line between two contiguous or adjacent numbers. On the layout, we see the chip placed between numbers 6 and 9 as a split bet, covering both numbers. The chip between 5 and 6 is also a split bet.

If either number comes up on a split bet, the player wins at 17-1. Split bets give the player double the chance to win, at just under half the payoff. Any two numbers may be split, as long as there is a line separating them. 0 and 00 may also be bet as a split number, either by putting a chip between these numbers, or, if you can't reach the 0 and 00 box, by putting one on the line between the second and third dozens.

Trio Bets

Three numbers bet; pays 11-1.

A **trio bet** can be made by placing a chip on the line separating the dozens betting area from the columns of numbers. The chip on the number 13 line in the layout below will cover the numbers 13, 14 and 15.

13	14	15

When a player makes a trio bet, he has covered three consecutive numbers. If any of those numbers comes up on the wheel, he receives a payoff of 11-1.

As you can see from the layout, the numbers that can be covered with a trio bet include 1, 2 and 3; 10, 11 and 12; 25, 26 and 27, and other similarly ordered groups.

The house advantage on this bet is still 5.26%

Corner Bets

Four numbers bet; pays 8-1.

A **corner bet** is made when a chip is placed at the point where four numbers converge, in exactly that corner. This type of bet is shown on the layout below, where the chip is placed between the numbers 23, 24, 26 and 27. If any of those numbers come up on the next spin of the wheel, the payoff will be 8-1. This wager is pretty versatile and can be used to cover various groups of four numbers, such as 2, 3, 5 and 6; 7, 8, 10 and 11; 22, 23, 25 and 26; and 32, 33, 35 and 36, among others.

The corner bet gives the house its usual 5.26% advantage.

Five-Number Bet

Five numbers bet; pays 6-1.

A **five-number bet** can be made only one way, and it covers the numbers 0, 00, 1, 2 and 3. A player makes such a bet by placing his chip at the convergence of the line separating the 0 and 00 and the line separating these numbers from the 1, 2 and 3. After noting where the chip goes, forget about this bet. It gives the house an advantage of 7.89%, and is therefore the *worst bet* on the entire roulette layout.

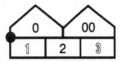

Since the French wheel contains only 0, not 00, this bet can't be made on that wheel. Take my advice—never make this bet at all.

Six-Number Bet

Six numbers bet; pays 5-1.

For a **six-number bet**, place the chip on the outside line separating the dozens bets from the inside numbers, at a point where this line crosses a line perpendicular to it that separates the six numbers we want to bet on. You can see an example of this bet in the layout diagrammed below.

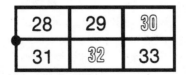

In the diagram, this chip is placed so that the numbers 28, 29, 30, 31, 32 and 33 are covered. Thus one chip covers all six numbers. If any of those numbers hit, the bet will be paid off at 5-1.

There are eleven possible ways to make this six-number bet running up and down the side of the layout. Since a six-number bet covers so many numbers at once and yields a good 5-1 payoff, it's very popular.

The house edge on this wager is 5.26%.

A final note on these wagers: no matter how you make them and how many chips you risk, as long as you avoid the five-number bet, the house edge will never be anything other than 5.26%.

With all of these wagers, the player may make several bets of the same kind, covering several numbers. He may also make combinations of bets that cover as many numbers as he wishes, using as many chips as he cares to risk, provided that the total amount he bets is within the house limit on wagers.

Outside Bets

The bets we'll now cover are made outside the 1-36, 0 and 00 numbered area. They are therefore considered **outside bets**.

There are three types of bets here. First, there are the even money wagers, then the dozens bets, and finally the column bets. We'll discuss each in turn.

1st 12		2nd 12		3rd 12	
1to18	EVEN	◇ ◆		ODD	19to36

The Even Money Bets

There are three possible types of bets that one can make for even money: high-low, odd-even, or red-black. Of course, a player can make wagers on each of these choices, betting, for example, odd, red and high.

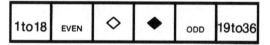

When a player bets on even money choices, the house wins automatically if the ball lands in the 0 or 00. There's one exception to this rule, and it takes place in Atlantic City or anywhere else where there's a **surrender rule**.

Let's discuss this rule now. If the number coming up is 0 or 00 in a place where surrender is allowed, the casino will allow you to remove *one-half of your bet*. In other words, you're surrendering just half your bet.

The European casinos go one step further.

In those casinos, the rule in effect is called the **en prison rule**. You can either surrender half your bet, or you can allow your bet to be "imprisoned" for one more spin. If your choice then comes up, your bet stays intact. However, you don't win; you just get your bet back. In Atlantic City you can only surrender.

In the Nevada casinos, neither rule is in effect. There, if you bet on any even money choice and the 0 or 00 comes up, you're out of luck. You lose your bet outright.

High-Low Bets

The first of the even money bets we'll discuss is the **high-low bet**. You can bet high (19-36) or low (1-18). If you bet high and any number from 19 to 36 comes up, you win your bet at even money, or 1-1. If you bet low and any number from 1-18 comes up, again, you win even money.

Odd-Even

If you bet odd, then if any odd number comes up on the next spin of the wheel, you win your wager at even money, or 1-1. If you bet even, then similarly, if any even number comes up, your bet is paid off at even money. Remember, however, that the numbers 0 and 00 are losers for this kind of bet, just as they are for all bets which payoff at even money.

Red-Black

There are eighteen red numbers and eighteen black numbers, so the chances of a red or black number coming up on the next spin of the wheel are equal. If you bet on red, you will be paid off at even money, or 1-1, if a red number comes up. If you bet black, you win even money if a black number comes up.

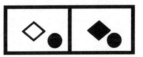

The layout diagrams show where you make your wagers for these even money choices. You can bet any amount up to the house limit, which is usually higher for even money choices than for the inside numbers, because the payoff is only at even money.

These even money choices are the heart of many roulette systems, and we'll cover a few in the later sections of this book. We'll show how they work, and we'll also explain their pitfalls.

Dozens Bets

These bets are paid off at 2-1, and there are three ways to bet them. You can bet on the first dozen, the second dozen or the third dozen. The first dozen covers numbers 1-12. On the layouts, it's often called the 1st 12. The numbers from 13-24 comprise the second dozen, which is known as the 2nd 12. Finally, there's the third dozen, from 25-36, which is known as the 3rd 12.

With each of those bets, a player is covering twelve numbers. Some players bet on two dozens at once, giving themselves twenty-four numbers. On these bets, as on the even-number wagers and the columns wagers, the house edge is always 5.26%.

When a 0 or 00 comes up, you have an automatic loser. These numbers aren't included in the dozens bets, and there is no surrender or *en prison* rule covering them in any casino.

The layout diagram above shows how to make these wagers, and where to place the chip or chips you bet. The house limit on these bets is higher than those on the inside numbers.

Columns Bet

These bets are made at the head of each column directly opposite 0 and 00 on the layout. A bet on a particular column covers twelve numbers, some red and some black.

3	6	9	12	15	18	21	24	27	30	33	36	2-1
2	5	8	11	14	17	20	23	26	29	32	35	2-1
1	4	7	10	13	16	19	22	25	28	31	34	2-1

The payoff is at 2-1 for each column bet, but the 0 and 00 aren't included in any column. If they come up, your column bet is lost. There is no surrender or *en prison* rule on column wagers.

The house edge is 5.26% on all column bets.

We have discussed the *en prison* and surrender rules on even money wagers. The house edge without these rules is 5.26% on all even money wagers, as well as on the dozens and columns bets. With the *en prison* and surrender rules, the house advantage drops to 2.70% *on only the even money wagers*.

Recapitulation of Bets and Payoffs	
Single Number	35-1
Two Numbers	17-1
Three Numbers	11-1
Four Numbers	8-1
Five Numbers	6-1
Six Numbers	5-1
Column	2-1
Dozen	2-1
Odd-Even*	1-1
Red-Black*	1-1
High-Low*	1-1

All of the above bets give the house an advantage of 5.26%, except for the five-numbers bet, which gives the casino an advantage of 7.89%.
* When the surrender feature is allowed, the house advantage on these bets drops to 2.70%.

European Roulette

The European game and the American game are nearly the same. Besides the use of French terms, there are just two main differences. First, the European game uses only a single zero, in contrast to the zero and double zero played in America. Second, the European game incorporates the *en prison* rule that we discussed earlier.

Both the single zero and the *en prison* rule are beneficial to the players; they bring the casino advantage down to 1.35%.

The French wheel has spaces for thirty-seven numbers: the numerals 1-36, and the single 0. Red and black numbers alternate, but the placement of numbers is different than on the American wheel.

Like the American wheel, the French wheel contains a groove near its rim, where the *croupier* (dealer) places the ball, spinning it counter to the motion of the wheel. The ball hits metal buffers as it loses speed, and finally it falls into one of the pockets. Again, the pockets are separated from each other by metal sides.

The Layout

The European layout also differs from the American layout in two ways. The even money choices here are on opposite sides, rather than adjacent to each other. Also, the dozens bets can be made on two different sides of the layout. The wheel is above the box showing the 0.

Let's compare the European and the American bets, showing the different nomenclature.

European and American Nomenclature		
American Bet	**French Term**	**Odds**
Straight-Up (One Number)	En plein	35-1
Split (Two Numbers)	A cheval	17-1
Trio (Three Numbers)	Transversale	11-1
Corner (Four Numbers)	Carre	8-1
Six Numbers	Sixain	5-1
* Red-Black	Rouge-Noir	1-1
* High-Low	Passe-Manque	1-1
*Odd-Even	Impair-Pair	1-1
Column	Colonne	2-1
Dozen	Douzaine	2-1

* The *en prison* rule is in effect for these betting choices only.

When you make dozens bets, you should realize that the first dozen (1-12) is marked as **P12** on the layout. The "P" stands for **Première**, a French word meaning "first." The second dozen (13-24) is called **M12**, for **Moyenne**, which means "middle." The third dozen is called **D12**, for **Derniére**, or "last."

To review, the *en prison* rule can be summarized as follows: when a 0 comes up on the wheel, the player's bet isn't lost. He now must make a choice: either he can surrender half his wager and keep the other half (a move known as **partage**), or his bet can be imprisoned for another spin, and, if it wins, he then loses nothing and gains nothing for that spin. To differentiate this second option from an ordinary wager, the player's chip or chips are placed on the line that borders the betting area.

Since the house advantage with the *en prison* rule is 1.35%, the most advantageous bets for players at a European casino would be on the even money choices.

There are many special bets also available at European casinos. Most of them involve what the French call **voisins**, or neighbors. A player can make a *voisins* bet on any number on the wheel, meaning that he would have bet on that number and on the two numbers on either side of it. Such a bet would be a five-chip bet. A **voisins du zero** bet involves a nine-chip bet, with eight chips bet on splits and one chip on the trio 0-2-3.

There are a handful of other wagers that are special to the European wheel, and you'll hear these referred to by names like *finals*, *les tiers*, and *les orphelins*. These bets are rather complicated and tend to confuse beginning (and even some advanced) roulette players. We advise the player to concentrate instead on the even money choices and the simpler bets, such as corner bets or splits.

Strategies & Systems at Roulette

Because of the high house edge at the American wheel without the surrender rule (an edge of 5.26% minimum on all bets), roulette at such casinos is not a game that you'll want to play for very serious money. The strong house advantage is quite difficult to overcome in the long run.

If you do play roulette, try to limit your losses. When you find yourself winning, try to make a good score and then quit while you're ahead. That's a philosophy that can't be beaten when gambling.

Getting Your Roulette Chips

When you first come to a table, you should ask the dealer what the minimum bets are at that particular table. If they're too high for your pocketbook, then don't play there. *Don't ever gamble with money you can't afford to lose, either financially or emotionally.*

Different casinos have different minimum bet limits. They also have different standard valuations for their chips. When chips are valued at $1, a stack of twenty chips will cost you $20. Some casinos will value their chips at 50¢, in which case you pay just $10 for the same stack of twenty. Some casinos will even value their chips at a 25¢ standard, which means that a stack of twenty chips would cost you $5. You can figure out the standard valuation by finding out what a stack of chips will cost you.

If you feel comfortable with the amount of money you're going to risk, you should now ask the dealer about minimum bets. Find out the minimum bet allowed for the inside as well as the outside numbers. Remember, the inside numbers are all the numbers (from 1-36 plus the 0 and 00) that can be bet as one, two, three, four or six number bets. The outside bets are those that pay off at even money, plus the dozens and the columns wagers.

Even when the chips cost 25¢ each, the casino might require a minimum outside bet of $1, and a minimum inside bet of 25¢ on any choice but only with at least four chips in play at the same time. In other words, you won't necessarily be allowed to place just one chip on one inside betting proposition. You might have to put down at least four on one or several betting choices, which would mean that you'd be risking a dollar each spin after all.

These practices are fairly standard in casinos, so be sure that your bankroll can handle them. If you're at a table with a $1 valuation for the chips, and you must bet four (sometimes it's even five) chips at once on the inside propositions, then you may be out of your original stake after just a few losses.

What Bets to Make

If you're playing at a standard American table, with the 0 and 00 and no surrender rule, then all your bets will give the house the same advantage of 5.26% (except for the five-number wager—0, 00, 1, 2 and 3—where the house advantage is even higher).

The higher the odds, the less likely you'll win. The lower the odds, the more often you'll win. Thus if you bet only on single numbers as straight-up bets, you'll get 35-1 for a win, but the odds are 37-1 against your winning.

On the other hand, if you bet on the even money choices, the odds against winning are only 20-18. You have 18 numbers working for you and 20 working against you, including the 0 and 00. Obviously you will theoretically win 18 out of 38 times, or much more often than 1 out of 37 times, as when betting a straight-up number.

The payoff is much less, of course: only even money. You must therefore use your discretion when making bets. Are you the type who wants to take a shot at a big payoff, or do you want to conserve your betting capital and hope to get a little bit ahead? It's your choice; the odds are the same where house percentage is concerned.

There are ways to compromise. You can make six-number bets and cover a large variety of numbers while still getting a good payoff. You can bet a key number straight-up, and then surround it with corner and trio bets. Many possibilities are available at the roulette table, and the choices are yours.

When you're playing at a table that allows surrender, you should by all means concentrate on the even money betting propositions. They cut the house edge in half, so why not take advantage? The same holds true when betting in a European game, since they incorporate the *en prison* rule. Bet on the even money choices. You get a second chance at winning back your bet when a 0 shows, and the house edge on this bet is down to 1.35%.

Betting Systems

The most well known, but also the most treacherous, systems to play are the Martingale and the Grand Martingale. The Martingale is often played by novices who feel that sooner or later their choice is going to come up, and to rationalize their bets, they call upon the *law of averages*.

Here's how the Martingale system works. It's really nothing more than a doubling up system. After a loss, you double your bet till you win. For example, let's suppose you bet $1. You lose. Then you bet $2. You lose. You bet $4. You lose. You bet $8. You win.

Having won, you start all over again with a $1 wager. How much can you win with this system? Well, when you finish a sequence of doubling up with a win, you are ahead only $1. Here's why:

Bet	Total Loss
$1	$1
$2	$3
$4	$7

At this point, you're behind $7. Then when you bet $8 and win, you win $8. Now you're ahead $1. Even if the bets escalate to $16, $32, $64, $128 and $256, when you finally win, you win $1. Imagine betting $256 to win $1! That's what this system is all about.

The Grand Martingale is even tougher. After each loss you add a unit to the bet, so that you win more than $1 when you finally win. The loss sequence, though, is $1, $3, $7, $15, and so forth, which can lead to astronomical losses in a very short time. If you're going to play these systems, you'd better have an awfully large bankroll to finance all your potential losses. It's better to avoid them.

The systems players who are die-hards think that the doubling up method will win because of the law of averages. After they've lost five bets on red, they feel that red is overdue because of the *law of averages*.

What they don't know is that there is no law of averages. There is only the law of large numbers, which roughly states that the more events played, the closer to the theoretical norm the result will be.

At the time the systems player is hoping for red to come up, he doesn't know that after a million spins of the wheel (even excluding the 0 and 00), red could have come up 521,202 times and black could have come up 478,798 times. Black still has a long way to go to catch up. In fact, it may never catch up, though it will come closer to the 50% norm as time goes by and there are several million more spins of the wheel.

If you want to play a betting system, play a very conservative one. For example, you might bet $1, and if it loses, bet $2. If that loses, you just want to break even, so you bet $3. If that loses, you've lost $6. You stop and restart with a $1 bet, hoping to win during the first two spins enough times to make up for the loss. Of course, you're not going to get rich that way, but you won't be losing your bankroll with one run of bad luck.

Since roulette is a leisurely game where you can sit down comfortably and make bets between spins of the wheel without much pressure, we suggest that you buy two stacks of chips and have fun playing. Hope to make some money through luck.

My best advice is to play some of your favorite numbers, make a few corner bets, and maybe some even number wagers. Enjoy yourself. If you have some luck, you can win big.

Money Management

Money management is always important in gambling. It means managing your gambling stake so that it not only can last a long time, but also will give you the chance of winning. For purposes of playing roulette, I'd suggest getting two stacks of chips only if you can afford to take such a risk. Play with the standard valuations. Now you have forty chips to bet. To make them last, you might pick a few favorite numbers and cover them with corner or six-number bets, thus giving yourself a good chance of picking up a winning number. At the same time, place a chip on two favorite numbers. If they hit, you're getting 35-1.

In the long run, try to double your stake. If you can do that, you're doing well at roulette. You've made a nice win, and it's time to leave the table. If your luck turns the other way and you lose, then don't reach into your pocket for more cash. Set your loss limits when you sit down at the table: two stacks and that's all you'll lose.

In this way, you'll have a shot at winning some money, some fun gambling, and not too much to lose.

Good luck!

Glossary of Roulette Terms

1st 12—The first twelve numbers on the layout, or 1-12. Known in French as **P12**.

2nd 12—The second twelve numbers on the layout, or 13-24. Known in French as **M12**.

3rd 12—The third twelve numbers on the layout, or 25-36. Known in French as **D12**.

American Wheel—The roulette wheel containing a 0 and 00.

Ball—The white, plastic object used in roulette, which is spun against the wheel's rotation to create a random spin.

Column Bet—A bet on one of the three columns on the roulette layout, each of which contains twelve numbers and is paid off at 2-1.

Combination Bet—A wager such as a corner bet, in which the bettor covers several inside numbers with just one chip or stack of chips.

Corner Bet—An inside bet in which the bettor uses one chip or stack of chips to cover four numbers at once. Also known as a **Four-Numbers Bet.**

Croupier—The French term for the employee who runs the roulette game.

D12—See **3rd 12**.

Derniére—The French word for "last."

Double Zero—See **Zero**.

Dozens Bet—A wager on either the first, second, or third dozen numbers on the layout.

En Prison Rule—A rule stating that when a 0 or 00 comes up, the player has the option of giving up half his bet or imprisoning the bet for one more spin. If the player's choice comes up on that next spin, nothing is won, but the bet is not lost. Also known as the **Surrender Rule**.

Even Money Bets—Bets paid off at even money, which include **High-Low**, **Odd-Even**, and **Red-Black**.

Five-Number Bet—A wager covering the 0, 00, 1, 2 and 3 which pays off at 6-1 and gives the house an advantage of 7.89%.

French Wheel—The standard wheel used in

Europe, containing a single zero.

High-Low Bet—An even money bet that the next spin will come up either high (19-36) or low (1-18), depending on whether the bettor has wagered on high or low.

Inside Bet—A wager on any of the numbers, or combinations of numbers, including 0 and 00.

Layout—The printed surface showing all the wagers that can be made in roulette, on which players place their bets.

M12—See **2nd 12**.

Martingale System—A doubling-up system after each loss.

Moyenne—The French word for "middle."

Odd-Even Bet—An even money wager that the next spin will come up the way the player bet it, either an odd or even number.

Outside Bet—A wager on either the dozens, columns or even money choices.

P12—See **1st 12**.

Partage—A French term referring to the surrender of a bet under the *en prison* rule.

Première—The French word for "first."

Rake—A tool in European roulette used to collect and pay off chips.

Red-Black Bet—A wager paid off at even money on either the red or black numbers.

Separators—The metal dividers separating

different pockets on the roulette wheel.

Six-Number Bet—A bet covering six inside numbers with one chip or stack of chips, paid off at 5-1.

Split Bet—A bet covering two numbers with one chip or stack of chips, paid off at 17-1.

Straight-Up Bet—A wager on just one number on the layout, paid off at 35-1.

Surrender Rule—See **En Prison Rule**.

Trio Bet—An inside bet covering three numbers at one time with one chip or stack of chips, paid off at 11-1.

Voisons—The French term for neighbors, referring to neighboring numbers on the French wheel.

Voisons du Zero—A nine-chip bet involving splits and 0-2-3.

Zero, Double Zero—Numbers on the wheel in addition to the regular 1-36 numerals; these allow the casino to have an edge over the players. Also called **House Numbers.**

One Final Word

Well, there you have it, a world of information presented to you on how to win at gambling. We all gamble not only to enjoy ourselves, but also to win. If you follow my advice, you'll be doing more of both every time you place your bets. After all, winning is more fun.

However, remember to gamble intelligently, and never risk money if losing it hurts you financially or emotionally. You're gambling to be a winner, and I mean that in more ways than one. This book is written not to encourage gambling, but rather to make you as informed as possible and give you every chance to make the best bets should you choose to gamble.

No matter what game you intend to play, I hope that my book has helped you become a better player, and that now, armed with powerful information, you will be a winner at gambling.

Go beat the odds!

THE CARDOZA CRAPS MASTER

3 Big Strategies! Exclusive Offer! - Not Available Anywhere Else

At last, the **secrets** of the **Grande-Gold Power Sweep**, **Molliere's Monte Carlo Turnaround** and the **Montarde-D'Girard Double Reverse** - three big strategies - are made available for the **first time anywhere**! These powerful strategies are designed for the serious craps player, one wishing to bring the best odds and strategies to hot, cold & choppy tables.

1. The Grande-Gold Power Sweep (Hot Table Strategy)–This **dynamic strategy** takes maximum advantage of hot tables and shows the player methods of amassing small **fortunes quickly** when numbers are being thrown fast and furious. The Grande-Gold stresses aggressive betting on wagers the house has no edge on! This previously unreleased strategy will make you a powerhouse at a hot table.

2. Molliere's Monte Carlo Turnaround (Cold Table Strategy)–For the player who likes betting against the dice, **Molliere's Monte Carlo** Turnaround shows how to turn a cold table into hot cash. Favored by an exclusive circle of professionals who will play nothing else, the uniqueness of this strongman strategy is that the vast majority of bets **give absolutely nothing away to the casino**!

3. The Montarde-D'Girard Double Reverse (Choppy Table Strategy)– This **new** strategy is the **latest development** and the **most exciting strategy** to be designed in recent years. **Learn how** to play the optimum strategies against the tables when the dice run hot and cold (a choppy table) with no apparent reason. **The Montarde-d'Girard Double Reverse** shows you how you can **generate big profits** while other players are ground out by choppy dice. The majority of our bets give nothing away to the casino!

BONUS!!! - Order now, and receive **The Craps Master-Professional Money Management Formula** ($15 value) **absolutely free**! Necessary for serious players and **used by the pros**, the it features the unique **stop-loss ladder** To order send ~~$75~~ $50 by check or money order to: <u>Cardoza Publishing</u>,

PROFESSIONAL VIDEO POKER STRATEGY
Win at Video Poker - With the Odds!

At last, for the **first time**, and for **serious players only**, the GRI **Professional Video Poker** strategy is released so you too can play to win! **You read it right** - this strategy gives you the **mathematical advantage** over the casino and what's more, it's **easy to learn**!

PROFESSIONAL STRATEGY SHOWS HOW TO WIN WITH THE ODDS

This **powerhouse strategy**, played for **big profits** by an **exclusive** circle of **professionals**, is now made available to you! You too can win - with the odds - and this **winning strategy** shows you how!

HOW TO PLAY FOR A PROFIT

You'll learn the **key factors** to play on a **pro level**: which machines will turn you a profit, break-even and win rates, hands per hour and average win per hour charts, time value, team play and more! You'll also learn big play strategy, alternate jackpot play, high and low jackpot play and key strategies to follow.

WINNING STRATEGIES FOR ALL MACHINES

This **comprehensive, advanced pro package** not only shows you how to win money at the 8-5 progressives, but also, the **winning strategies** for 10s or better, deuces wild, joker's wild, flat-top, progressive and special options features.

BE A WINNER IN JUST ONE DAY

In just one day, after learning our strategy, you will have the skills to **consistently win money** at video poker - with the odds.

BONUS - PROFESSIONAL PROFIT EXPECTANCY FORMULA

$15 Value! For serious players, we're including this bonus essay which discusses the profit expectancy principles of video poker and how to relate them to real dollars and cents in your game.

   To order, send $50 by check or money order to Cardoza Publishing

Baccarat Master Card Counter
NEW WINNING STRATEGY!

For the **first time**, Gambling Research Institute releases the **latest winning techniques** at baccarat. This **exciting** strategy, played by big money players in Monte Carlo and other exclusive locations, is based on principles that have made insiders and pros **hundreds of thousands of dollars** counting cards at blackjack - card counting!

NEW WINNING APPROACH

This brand **new** strategy now applies card counting to baccarat to give you a **new winning approach,** and is designed so that any player, with just a little effort, can successfully take on the casinos at their own game - and win!

SIMPLE TO USE, EASY TO MASTER

You learn how to count cards for baccarat without the mental effort needed for blackjack! No need to memorize numbers - keep the count on the scorepad. Easy-to-use, play the strategy while enjoying the game!

LEARN WHEN TO BET BANKER, WHEN TO BET PLAYER

No longer will you make bets on hunches and guesses - use the GRI Baccarat Master Card Counter to determine when to bet Player and when to bet Banker. You learn the basic counts (running and true), deck favorability, when to increase bets and much more in this **winning strategy**.

LEARN TO WIN IN JUST ONE SITTING

That's right! After **just one sitting** you'll be able to successfully learn this powerhouse strategy and use it to your advantage at the baccarat table. Be the best baccarat player at the table - the one playing the odds to **win**! Baccarat can be beaten. The Master Card Counter shows you how!

FREE BONUS!

Order now to receive **absolutely free**, <u>The Basics of Winning Baccarat</u>. One quick reading with this great primer shows you how to play and win.

CARDOZA SCHOOL OF BLACKJACK
- Home Instruction Course - $200 OFF! -

At last, after years of secrecy, the **previously unreleased** lesson plans, strategies and playing tactics formerly available only to members of the Cardoza School of Blackjack are now available - and at substantial savings. **Now**, you can **learn at home**, and at your own convenience. Like the full course given at the school, the home instruction course goes **step-by-step** over the winning concepts. We'll take you from layman to **pro**.

MASTER BLACKJACK - Learn what it takes to be a **master player**. Be a **powerhouse**, play with confidence, impunity, and **with the odds** on your side. Learn to be a **big winner** at blackjack.

MAXIMIZE WINNING SESSIONS - Take a good winning session and make a **blockbuster** out of it, but just as important, you'll learn to cut your losses. Learn exactly when to end a session. We cover everything from the psychological and emotional aspects of play to altered playing conditions (through the **eye of profitability**) to protection of big wins. The advice here could be worth **hundreds (or thousands) of dollars** in one session alone.

ADVANCED STRATEGIES - You'll learn the **latest** in advanced winning strategies. Learn about the **ten-factor**, the **Ace-factor**, the effects of rules variations, how to protect against dealer blackjacks, the winning strategies for single and multiple deck games and how each affects you; you'll learn the **true count**, the multiple deck true count variations, and much, much more.

And, of course, you receive the full Base Count Strategy package.

$200 OFF - LIMITED OFFER - The Cardoza School of Blackjack home instruction course, a $295 retail value (or $895 if taken at the school) is available now for just $95!!!

BONUS! - **Rush** your order in **now** for we're also including, **absolutely free**, the 1,000 word essays, "How to Disguise the Fact that You're an Expert", and "How Not to Get Barred". Among other **inside information** contained here, you'll learn about the psychology of pit bosses and how they spot counters.

To order, send $95 by check or money order to <u>Cardoza Publishing</u>: